# EASY TO MAKE
## CHRISTMAS CRAFTS

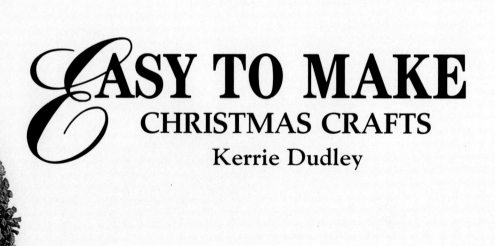

# EASY TO MAKE
## CHRISTMAS CRAFTS
### Kerrie Dudley

BROCKHAMPTON PRESS LONDON

First published in Great Britain in 1992
by Anaya Publishers Ltd, Strode House,
44-50 Osnaburgh Street, London NW1 3ND

This edition published 1995 by Brockhampton Press,
a member of Hodder Headline PLC Group

**Editor** Eve Harlow
**Design** by Design 23
**Photographer** Di Lewis
**Illustrator** Kate Simunek
**Artwork** Design 23

British Library Cataloguing in Publication Data

Dudley, Kerrie
Christmas crafts. – (Easy to make)
(Easy to Make Series)
1. Crafts. Christmas
I. Title    II. Series
ISBN 1-86019-134-7

Typeset by Servis Filmsetting Ltd, Manchester, UK
Colour reproduction by Columbia Offset, Singapore
Printed and bound in EC

# CONTENTS

# Introduction

*For the best-loved holiday of the year, what could be nicer than
having the house full of bright and jolly decorations*

Originally a pagan festival, coinciding
with the winter solstice in the northern
hemisphere, the practices of feasting,
decorating with evergreens and the giving
of gifts at the end of December were
encouraged by the Christian church as
part of the commemoration of the birth
of Jesus Christ. Now 25 December is
celebrated throughout the world and is
the best loved holiday of the year. Every
country has its own customs and
traditions, and I hope there are some
decorations in this book to complement
your festivities.

Whenever possible, I have used
materials which are freely available in
most households and would normally be
thrown away. Plastic bottles are
transformed into shiny golden bells,
colourful clowns and a smart Santa doll.
Other designs utilize acetate packaging,
cardboard tubes and old greetings cards.

Bringing evergreens into the home is an
age old custom in which, traditionally, the
foliage is used to represent life through
the long, dark winter days. Today, this
type of decoration is still hung inside or
outside the home, and there are two
simple designs for a welcoming wreath
and a greenery swag. Evergreens fill the
house with a sweet fragrance which no
artificial decoration can provide. The
chapter 'Christmas at home' also includes
other decorations to display around your
home to fill it with seasonal cheer.

**The tradition of the tree**
In many countries, even those basking in
sunshine in December, there are large
decorated trees in city squares where
people gather to sing carols in celebration
of the Holy birth. In the home, the tree is
usually the focal point of the decorations,
and trimming the tree has become a ritual
for many families, whether it be in a
sophisticated colour scheme or a riot of
colour and glitter. Bringing home the tree
and unwrapping the stored away
decorations is all part of the fun, for
adults and children alike. In some
countries, the family makes all the
decorations, adding to them each year,
and even have a special day for 'cutting
and sticking'. There are lots of little
decorations in the chapter 'Trim the tree'
including a bright golden star for the top
of your tree.

Whether your tradition is for turkey
and plum pudding, or roast lamb and
fresh fruit, the holiday is a time for
family feasts, and your party table will
look more attractive with some sparkling
decorations. There are several to choose
from in the chapter 'Top tables',
including a traditional Santa, a reindeer
and sleigh packed with gifts, and a row of
cheeky robins perched on a snow-
covered log.

## Gifts and greetings

This is also a time for sharing and giving. You will find decorations in this book which can be used as presents – little trees to brighten up an elderly neighbour's house or tree trims to boost the sales at a fund-raising bazaar. Add some fun to your gift wrapping also – top Granny's gift with a cheeky pompon snowman, or add some sparkle to Grandpa's present with a frizzy-haired little angel.

Christmas is also the time of year when we send greetings to friends, renew old acquaintances, and make contact with family members who live some distance away. What better way of sending that message than with a hand-made card that will be treasured?

In the 'Greetings' chapter there are several original card designs that will intrigue you – including two amusing 'wobbly' cards that are simple to make.

## Remembering Christmas

Christmas is, of course, special for children. Most of us remember our childhood Christmases as being full of excitement and fun – perhaps the large family gatherings with the house overflowing with aunts, uncles and cousins. Or waking up on Christmas morning to find a stocking or bag at the end of the bed, bulging with gifts – a sign that Santa had come during the night.

Although present day Christmases have perhaps become more sophisticated than those of old, this year's celebration need not be any less memorable for your children. Plan now to make it special with the whole family working together making the decorations. But, before you start, make sure you have a safe and happy holiday by reading my notes on safety.

## Safe and sure

The projects in this book are decorations rather than toys. Many have wire or other materials which could be pulled off by determined little fingers, so, if there are likely to be young children around at Christmas, keep all decorations out of reach.

Take care when making the decorations. Follow the instructions on adhesives and have the appropriate solvents ready in case of accidental spillage (check with Better techniques). Protect work surfaces when using craft knives, and keep your fingers clear of the cutting edge. Supervise children, especially where cutting is involved. When spraying adhesives or paints follow the instructions on the container, and always spray in a well-ventilated room.

Make sure all decorations are displayed safely and, in particular, not too close to an open fire. Many decorations, especially those made of paper, plastic and dried foliage are highly inflammable so never leave a naked flame unattended. Always replace a candle before it burns too low. Many evergreens, including their berries, are extremely toxic, so keep these well out of reach of young children.

# ONE

# Christmas at Home

# Door wreath

*Holly is used for this traditional wreath for the festive season. Hang it on an outside wall or door and it will stay fresh for days to welcome your guests.*

## Materials
18in (45cm) florists' foam ring
Holly, or other fresh evergreen
8 silk poinsettia flowers
Mini parcels
Gold thread
Florists' wire

## Preparation
1 Buy or cut holly only a day or two before making the wreath to ensure freshness.

2 Soak the ring in water and drain off the excess.

3 Make the mini parcels and tie a piece of gold thread to the top of each to make a long hanging loop.

Insert silk poinsettia flowers into the ring.

### Larger gift boxes
Draw the shape on squared paper with 10 squares to 1in (2.5cm). Copy this drawing on squared paper again with every original square as 4 squares, thus making the box four times bigger – 7 × 4in (17.5 × 10cm).

### Mini parcels
To make these decorative little ornaments you need thin card, giftwrap, narrow ribbon, all-purpose glue and double-sided tape.
　　Draw the box outline on this page and cut the shape from thin card. Score along the fold lines. Cut pieces of giftwrap 3 × 5in (7.5 × 12.5cm). Fold the card into a box shape, insert a tiny gift if you like, then stick the tabs. Wrap the box neatly in giftwrap and apply strips of double-sided tape to neaten the overlap and ends. Apply double-sided tape to ribbon, remove the paper and attach ribbon strips around the parcels. Make small bows to decorate.

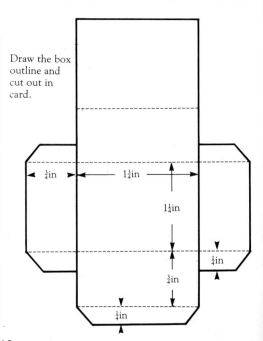

Draw the box outline and cut out in card.

$\frac{1}{4}$in  1$\frac{1}{4}$in

1$\frac{1}{4}$in

$\frac{1}{4}$in

$\frac{3}{4}$in

$\frac{1}{4}$in

## Working the design

**4** Work around the ring pushing pieces of holly into the florists' foam until the ring is completely covered.

**5** Insert the poinsettia flowers' stems into the florists' foam so that the flowers nestle amongst the holly.

**6** Bend a piece of florists' wire in half and thread this through the hanging loop of one mini parcel. Insert the wire into the ring so that the parcel hangs freely inside the wreath. Add other parcels in the same way.

# Festive garland

*A greenery swag looks attractive draped around the mantelpiece, a window or a door. Any fresh evergreen foliage can be used and it will fill the house with its fragrance.*

**Materials**

Conifer, or any evergreen foliage, cut in approximately 12in (30cm) lengths

Roll of florists' wire

1½in (4cm)-wide tartan ribbon, approximately 30in (75cm) for each bow

Small piece of 1in (2.5cm)-wide gold metallic ribbon for each of the bows' knots

Fresh foliage garlands can sometimes shrivel in centrally-heated rooms. Florists can provide artificial garlands that look real and, decorated with dried material and ribbon bows, they can be kept for several years. Moss garlands are also an ideal base for dried material and can be made very simply.

Cut a piece of wire netting to the required length and to about 12in (30cm) wide. Lay it on a flat surface. Make a long mound of damp sphagnum moss along the edge nearest to you. Roll the wire netting away from you and over the moss to form a roll. Fold in the ends of the roll. Leave the roll to dry completely before decorating it.

Decorate the garland with fir cones, dried seed heads, walnuts (glue a wire to the base), preserved beech leaves, dried red helichrysum flowers etc, plus red or gold ribbon bows. A few glittering Christmas tree baubles could also be added. Hang the garland from wires threaded through the ends.

**Preparation**

1 Buy or cut the evergreen foliage only a day or two before making the swag to ensure freshness.

2 Decide on the length of the swag according to where you intend to hang it and make enough bows to fix at approximately 15in (38cm) intervals along it.

**Working the design**

3 Wind the wire straight from the roll around each piece of evergreen in a continuous process, overlapping each new piece by at least three-quarters of its length over the previous one.

4 When the required length has been reached, fix the bows on to the swag with florists' wire.

Add foliage sprigs, overlapping each piece three-quarters of its length. Bind in place.

# Fabric wall wreath

*This festive-looking wreath is made from scraps of fabric and a wire coathanger. Use a mixture of plain and Christmas print fabric in colours to suit your décor.*

## Materials
Pieces of plain and Christmas print fabric (a 12in (30.5cm) piece of 45in (114cm)-wide fabric will make 7 puffs)
12in (30cm) of 36in (90cm)-wide wadding
Wire coathanger
Florists' wire

## Preparation
1 Use a pair of compasses to draw two circular card templates. 6in (15cm) and 3in (7.5cm) diameter. Cut out.

2 Using the templates cut 28 large circles from patterned fabric and 14 large circles from plain fabric. Make a tiny hole in the centre of each circle by folding it into quarters and snipping off the point.

3 Cut 42 small circles from wadding.

4 Use wire cutters to cut off the hook of the coathanger leaving about ½in (12mm) extending. Use pliers to untwist and then bend one of the ends back on itself. Form the hanger into a circle.

## Working the design
5 To make each puff, gather a fabric circle edge, place a wadding circle to the wrong side of the fabric, pull up the gathers tightly and fasten off the thread.

6 Push the puffs on to the hanger, alternating two patterned with one plain.

7 When the hanger is full, use pliers to bend the remaining end back on itself and bind the two ends together with wire. Stitch the puffs each side of the join together so that the join in the hanger cannot be seen.

8 Make a large fabric bow using an 8in (20cm) strip of 45in (114cm) wide fabric (refer to 'Making bows' in Better techniques). Stitch the bow in place.

9 Make a hanging loop from a piece of gold thread by tying each end to the wire hanger on each side of the top two puffs.

Place wadding circle to wrong side of fabric.

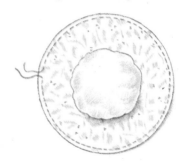

Pull up gathers tightly.

Push the puffs on to the wire.

# Doves mobile

*Doves made from felt are hung from a ring of ivy to make this charming Christmas mobile. Individual doves can be hung at the window or used as tree trims.*

**Materials**
10in (25cm)-diameter lampshade ring
Ivy (silk or natural)
1in (2.5cm)-wide white ribbon, 15in (38cm) for each bow
18in (45cm) square of white felt
Gold braid
Small amount of Terylene stuffing
Small amount of fusible web
Gold sewing thread
10 gold sequins
Florists' wire

## DOVES
**Preparation**
1 Iron fusible web on to the white felt for the wings.

2 Iron fusible web on to the back of sufficient gold braid to cover 5 pairs of wings.

3 Trace the dove's body shape and then the wing separately and make card templates.

**Working the design**
4 Draw around the wing template on the fusible web-backed felt and cut out 5 pairs of wings. Make sure you reverse the template for 5 of the wings when drawing around it.

5 In the same way cut out 5 pairs of wings from the fusible web-backed braid. Peel off the paper backing from the braid wings and iron them on to the felt side of the felt wings.

6 Use the body template to cut 10 body shapes in white felt with ½in (1cm) extra all round the 5 back pieces.

7 Position a wing on to each body shape, peel the paper backing from the wings and iron in place. Stitch wings in place using a machine zigzag stitch and gold thread.

8 Stitch front to back using a machine zigzag stitch and leaving a gap for stuffing. Stuff the dove lightly then zigzag stitch the opening.

9 Trim off the excess felt close to the stitching. Sew a gold sequin on each side of the head for eyes.

## IVY RING
**Preparation**
10 Make 5 white ribbon bows.

11 Twine ivy around the ring until it is completely covered.

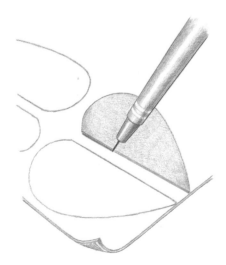

Make sure you reverse the template when cutting out the second wing.

## Working the design

**12** Tie four 20in (50cm) lengths of gold thread to the ring at equal intervals. Bring the ends together and tie a knot approximately 6in (15cm) from the ends, evenly balancing the ring.

**13** Tie another knot at the end of the threads, to form a hanging loop.

**14** Thread gold thread through the centre back of each dove above the wings so that the dove is balanced. Hang the 5 doves, evenly spaced, around the ring so that they are suspended about 6in (15cm) below the ivy.

**15** Fix a ribbon bow with florists' wire above each dove.

**Trace the body shape.**
**Trace the wing separately.**

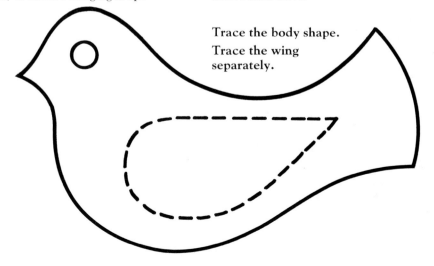

# Gold bells

*These large golden bells are made by recycling plastic bottles, so they are cheap to make and environmentally friendly. Use ozone-friendly car paint to colour the bells.*

**Materials**
**(for each bell)**
2 litre plastic fizzy drinks bottle
3 litre plastic drinks bottle
Gold spray car paint
36in (90cm) gold braid
6in (15cm) narrow gold cord
1 gold bauble
Approximately 7in (18cm) of ¼in (6mm) dowel
1 standard cork
Latex adhesive
All-purpose glue
Gold ribbon

**Preparation**
1 Using a craft knife, carefully cut the top 5½in (14cm) from the 2 litre bottle. Discard the bottom. Cut off the top ¾in (18mm) from the neck and discard.

2 Cut the top 4in (10cm) from the top of the 3 litre bottle. Discard the bottom.

3 Spray both bottle tops and the dowel with gold car paint, following the directions on the can. Several light layers, allowing the bottles to dry between coats, results in a better finish.

4 Make a ¼in (6mm) hole through the cork from top to bottom, and a small groove in each side (also from top to bottom) to take the cord. Using all-purpose glue, stick the ends of the 6in (15cm) length of cord each side of the cork so that it forms a hanging loop.

**Working the design**
5 Using all-purpose glue, stick the bottom of the 2 litre top to the 3 litre top. Allow to dry.

6 Using latex adhesive, stick gold braid around the bell at the join, and around the top and bottom.

7 Insert the cork, with the cord in place, into the top of the bell.

8 Using all-purpose glue, stick one end of the dowel into the top of the bauble. Feed the other end of the dowel up through the bell and push it through the cork so that the bauble just protrudes from the bottom. Cut off any excess dowel with a craft knife.

9 Make a large gold bow to hang above the bell.

---

**Small bells**
Some laundry detergent bottles have large, screw-on measuring caps and these are ideal for making bells for the tree. Glue a small plastic ring to the top. Spray-paint the cap gold inside and out. Spray-paint a 6in (15cm)-long piece of wire gold. Twist the wire ends through the hangers of small gold baubles for clappers. Bend the wire double and stick the clappers inside the cap with quick-drying adhesive. Tie 2 bells together with ¼in (6mm)-wide ribbon. These small bells also look good suspended inside a door wreath.

Picture bells are made in the same way. Cut suitable motifs from old Christmas cards to 2 × 1in (5 × 2.5cm) ovals. Stick a picture on each side of the bell. Stick gold braid round the pictures.

Stick the top of the smaller bottle to the
larger bottle.

Push the dowel up through the bell and into the
cork.

19

# Window flashers

*Hang these sparkling baubles in the window and they will flash in the light as they sway in the air currents. You could also make some to use as tree decorations.*

**Materials**
Assorted colours of sequin waste (20in (50cm) will make 3 baubles)
Medium-weight gold card
Gold Lurex thread; thin gold thread
All-purpose glue

**Preparation**
1 With a pair of compasses, draw a circle on card 3in (7.5cm) diameter. Cut out for a template.

2 Use the template to cut circles of sequin waste, two of the same colour for each bauble.

3 Trace the bauble pattern and make a card template. Cut 2 from gold card for each bauble.

**Working the design**
4 Stick a small loop of gold Lurex thread to the wrong side of one card bauble at the top. Spread glue on the wrong side of both card baubles.

5 Rotate one circle of sequin waste against the other until a floral pattern is formed. Sandwich the two pieces between the card baubles.

Cut the middle circles from the gold card baubles.

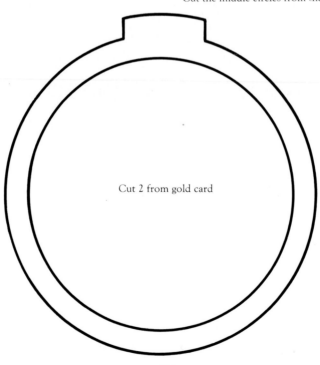

Cut 2 from gold card

**6** Put a weight (for example a thick book) on top of the bauble so that it dries flat.

**7** Use lengths of gold thread to hang the baubles in front of the window.

Trace suitable motifs – stars, trees etc – from greetings cards or giftwrap and cut them from heavy, two-sided foil. Add a hanger at the top. Suspend the shapes from nylon threads and hang the foil flashers against the window.

Rotate the circles of sequin waste until a pattern forms.

# Making holly

*These larger-than-life sized holly leaves are made from sheets of packaging acetate sprayed with green paint. As they are translucent, they display well against a window.*

**Materials**
Sheets of acetate approximately 8 × 6in
  (20 × 15cm)
Green spray car paint
1in (2.5cm) cotton pulp balls painted red
Thin florists' binding wire
Green florists' tape
Pipe cleaners
All-purpose glue
Ribbon

**Preparation**
1 Score the acetate sheets with veins using a sharp instrument such as a

skewer. Score the lines away from you in a continuous flowing movement. (Take care to protect the working surface.)

2 Glue a pipe cleaner into each cotton ball. When dry, use florists' tape to bind 3 balls together for berries.

**Working the design**
3 Draw the holly leaf pattern on squared paper and then cut the shape from the scored acetate sheet.

4 Gently bend the leaf up on each side of the central spine and then on each side of each vein, to form the holly leaf.

Holly leaf: scale 1 sq = 1in (2.5cm).

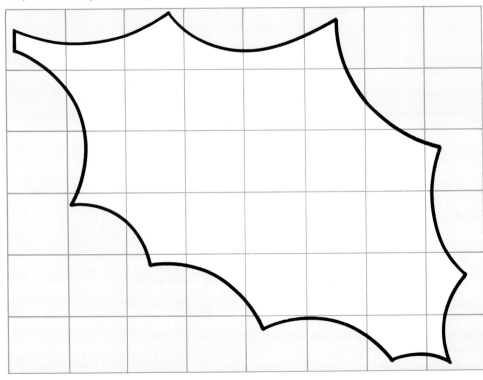

22

Score the acetate sheet with vein marks.

**6** Push a 6in (15cm) length of florists' wire through each leaf about 1in (2.5cm) from the end. Twist one end around the end of the leaf then the other end of the wire to make a stem.

**7** Use florists' wire to bind two leaves and a bunch of three berries together. Cover the wires with florists' tape. Display the holly with large ribbon bows. Several sprays of holly could be wired and displayed together.

**5** Spray the back of the leaves with green car paint, following the directions on the can. Several light layers allowing the leaves to dry between coats, results in a better finish. Do not spray the front, and the leaf will retain its shine.

Twist the end of the wire round the leaf then twist the wire ends together.

# TWO

# Trim the Tree

# Felt gift bags

*Children will love these bright little bags which are cut from felt.
For an extra little surprise, pop a few coins in each one
and watch their faces light up with joy.*

**Materials**
Red, green and white felt
Scraps of gold braid and ribbon
Fusible web

**Preparation**
1 Trace the shapes on to tracing (or
greaseproof) paper. Use the patterns to
cut two of each shape from felt, allowing
½in (1cm) all around.

2 Iron pieces of fusible web on to the
back of pieces of braid. Remove the
paper backing and iron braid on to the
front of each shape (see picture).

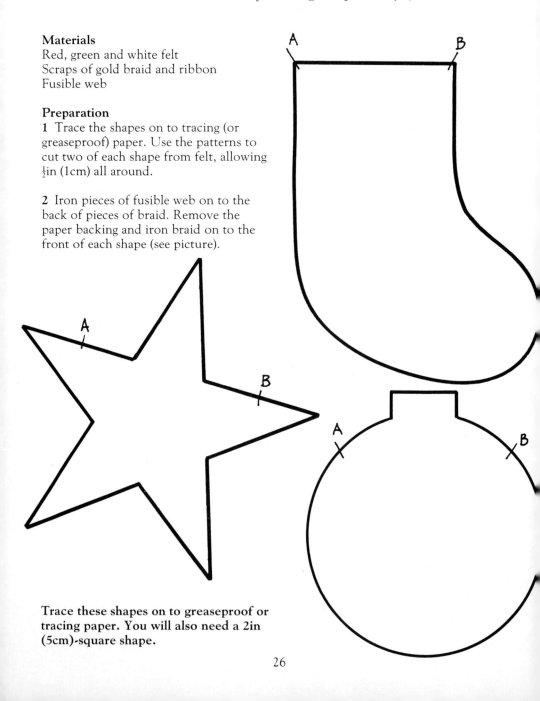

Trace these shapes on to greaseproof or
tracing paper. You will also need a 2in
(5cm)-square shape.

## Working the design

**3** Pin the paper pattern to a front piece then baste the front to the back. Stitch around the shape close to the pattern edge, leaving an opening (A-B on the patterns). Unpin the paper pattern.

**4** Trim round the bag close to the stitching and close to the pattern line where the seam is unstitched.

**5** Use fusible web to attach a loop of gold braid or ribbon at the top of each bag for a hanger.

# Candy canes in fabric

*These candy canes look good enough to eat but will last for years.*
*They can be hung on the tree or inside a door wreath*
*as a special greeting to your visitors.*

**Materials**
**(for each cane)**
6in (15cm) square of white felt
¼in (6mm)-wide red ribbon, 12in (30.5cm)
    long
1in (2.5cm)-wide green ribbon, 20in
    (50cm) long
Narrow silver ribbon
Small amount of toy filling
Fusible web

**Preparation**
1 Trace the cane shape on to tracing (or greaseproof) paper. Use the pattern to cut the shape twice from felt allowing ½in (1cm) all around.

2 Iron pieces of fusible web on to the back of the red ribbon. Peel off the paper backing and iron the ribbon in diagonal stripes on to the front of the cane.

**Working the design**
3 Pin the pattern piece to one cane piece, then baste front and back together, pinning the ends of a 5in (12.5cm) length of silver ribbon between the layers at the top for a hanger.

4 Stitch round the shape, close to the edge, leaving an opening for stuffing. Unpin the pattern.

5 Stuff the cane lightly and close the open seam with back stitches.

Use the candy cane shape to make tree decorations from slow-bake modelling clay. Remember to pierce a hole for a hanger before baking.

6 Trim round the candy cane, close to the stitching.

7 Make a green ribbon bow and sew it to the cane at an angle (see picture).

insert ends of hanging loop

leave opening

**Trace this cane shape on to greaseproof or tracing paper.**

# Tree-top ornament

*No tree is complete without its crowning glory. This sparkling golden star is perfect for the top of the tree and is simple to create from card and braid.*

**Materials**
10 × 20in (25 × 50cm) piece of gold card
2½in (6cm) piece of cardboard tube
Small piece of gold paper (to cover the
  tube)
40in (100cm) of narrow gold braid.
Gold Lurex thread
All-purpose glue
Double-sided tape
Clear sticky tape

**Preparation**
1 Cut the gold card into 2 pieces 10in
(25cm) square. Use a pair of compasses
to draw a circle 5in (12.5cm) radius on
the wrong side of one piece of the gold
card. With a ruler and protractor, draw
lines from the centre to each of the 5
points of the star (each angle is 72°).

2 Draw a line between every other point.
Cut out the star. Use this as a template to
cut a second star for the back from the
other piece of gold card.

3 Cover the tube with gold paper.

**Working the design**
4 On the right side of the front star score
the lines from the centre to the points,
and on the wrong side, score the lines
from the centre to the angles between the
points.

5 Bend the star carefully along the scored
lines to form its sculptured shape.

6 Flatten out the star to decorate it. Cut
thin strips of double-sided tape and
attach to the back of the braid. Attach a
small piece of double-sided tape at each
point and stretch lengths of Lurex thread

between the point and the opposite angle
between points, securing the Lurex
thread at the back of the star with sticky
tape. Remove the paper backing from the
braid and stick strips of braid along the
edges of the star.

7 Bend the star back into shape.

8 The back star is scored and folded in
the opposite way so that it fits into the
back of the decorated star. Glue in place.

9 Fix the gold covered tube to the back
of the star so that it will fit over the top
of the tree.

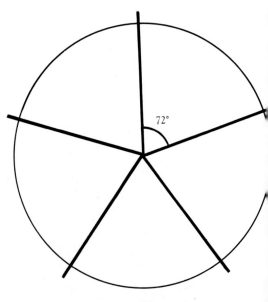

Draw lines from the centre with 72° angles.

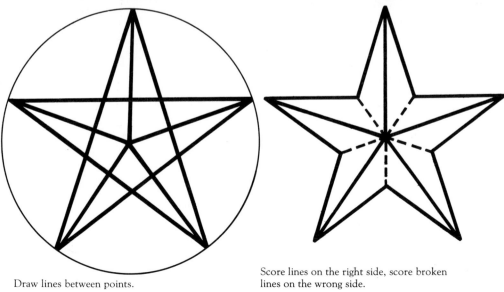

Draw lines between points.

Score lines on the right side, score broken lines on the wrong side.

31

# Tree skirt

*With this bright Christmas tree skirt, there will still be parcels around the tree when all the presents have been opened. The instructions can be adapted to suit any size tree.*

## Materials
36in (90cm) piece of pattern paper
36in (90cm) square each of red felt and
   green felt
Small pieces of felt in assorted colours
Fusible web
Scraps of ribbon and braid

## Preparation
1 Draw a 34in (86cm)-diameter circle on the paper. Draw an inner circle, 7in (18cm) diameter.

2 Cut out the paper ring and use this as a template to draw the shape on red felt using a soft pencil. Draw 2 lines, ¼in (6mm) apart, between the inner and outer circle for the back opening. (Do not cut the skirt out at this stage as the edge tends to become rather stretched during the making.)

3 Make card templates for the parcels with the following measurements:
   3 × 5in (7.5 × 12.5cm)
   1½ × 5in (4 × 12.5cm)
   3 × 3in (7.5 × 7.5cm)
   2 × 3in (5 × 7.5cm)
   2 × 2in (5 × 5cm)
   1 × 2in (2.5 × 5cm)

4 Holding the templates on felt, cut out the parcels. Cut 10–15 of each size.

5 Cut thin strips of fusible web and iron on to the back of pieces of ribbon and braid. Remove the paper backing and iron the ribbon and braid to the felt parcel shapes. Do not add bows at this stage.

## Working the design
6 Iron pieces of fusible web on to the back of the parcels. Position the parcels on the red felt, remove the paper backing and iron in place.

7 Work machine zigzag stitch round the edges of each parcel.

8 Cut out the skirt and pin to the green felt square. Work a close zigzag machine stitch all around the inner and outer edges of the skirt and along both edges of the back opening, catching the end of a 12in (30cm) length of red ribbon on each side of the opening for the ties.

9 Cut off the excess green felt close to the stitching. Press the skirt. Sew, or use fusible web, to add bows, felt holly leaves etc to decorate the parcels.

Work close zigzag stitch all round the inner and outer edges catching in the ribbon tie ends.

# Pretty angels

*These little angels can be made in minutes and are perfect for children to make with a minimum of mess. Use the angels for the tree, or perhaps to make a seasonal mobile.*

## Materials
### (for one angel)
1in (2.5cm) cotton pulp ball, painted pink
Gold foil paper
Paper doyleys
4in (10cm) piece of thick gold cord
6in (15cm) piece of thin gold braid or
    ribbon
Gold thread
Black felt tip pen
All-purpose glue

## Preparation
1 Use a pair of compasses to draw a semi-circle on gold foil paper 3in (7.5cm) radius. Cut out and form into a cone, overlapping and sticking about 1¼in (3cm) at the base.

## Working the design
2 Wrap a piece of doyley around the cone and stick in place.

3 Enlarge the hole slightly at the base of the cotton ball, fill with glue and push the ball on to the point of the cone.

4 To make the hair, tie a piece of gold thread around the centre of a 4in (10cm) length of gold cord. Unravel the ends of the cord and stick to the head so that the hair falls around the sides and back of the head.

5 Draw black eyes on the face.

6 Cut a 6in (15cm) length of thin gold braid (or ribbon) and form it into a figure-of-eight with one circle approximately ¾in (18mm) diameter for the halo and the other larger to form the hanging loop. Stick the centre of the 8 to the back of the head.

Glue unravelled gold cord to the cotton ball head.

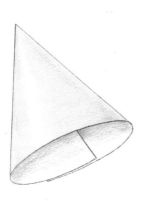

Form the foil semi-circle into a cone, glueing the overlap.

Glue gold braid to the head for a halo and hanging loop.

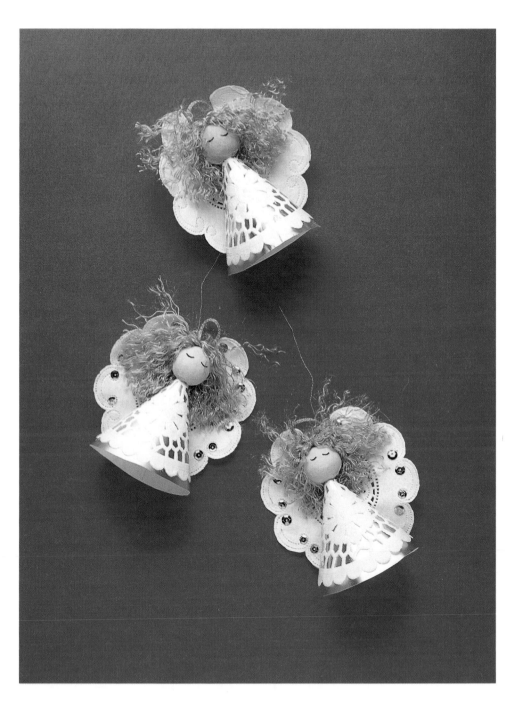

**7** Cut out the centre section of a white or gold paper doyley to make the wings. Cut in halves and stick each to the back of the cone so that the wings overlap at the base and are approximately $\frac{3}{4}$in (18mm) apart at the top.

Cut the cone from blue or red paper, stick on a white paper doyley surplice and sleeves. Omit the halo and wings to make a choir boy.

# Santa and snowman

*Wool pompon toys make ideal tree decorations but they can also be used to make a wrapped gift look special. Children could make them for gifts for family and friends.*

## SNOWMAN

### Materials
White DK knitting wool
Scraps of black, red and orange felt
Small piece of gold braid or ribbon
Gold Lurex thread
Thin card
Latex adhesive

### Preparation
1  Trace the figure-of-eight and cut 2 from card.

2  Trace the hat brim, eyes, mouth and nose patterns and cut out in black, red and orange felt.

3  Cut a ¾in (18mm) radius circle of black felt for the top of the hat, and a 1 × 4½in (2.5 × 11cm) piece of black felt for the sides. Cut a ½ × 9in (12mm × 23cm) piece of red felt for the scarf.

### Working the design
4  Holding the two figure-of-eight pieces of card together, wind white wool over the middle to hold them together.

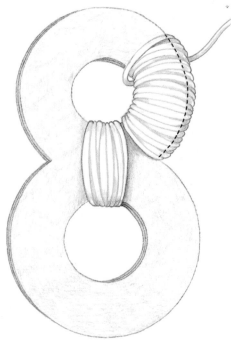

**Trace this figure-of-eight shape for a template. Holding 2 shapes together, wind wool over until the holes are filled. (Refer to the instructions for colours.)**

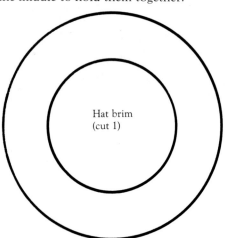

Hat brim
(cut 1)

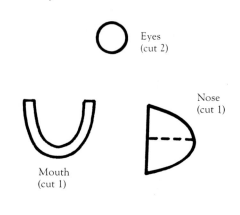

Eyes
(cut 2)

Mouth
(cut 1)

Nose
(cut 1)

**5** Continue to wind wool around the top and bottom sections of the 8 until both holes are completely filled.

**6** Using sharp, pointed scissors, snip through the wool round the edges until the card is exposed. Use a bodkin or large-eyed darning needle to thread a length of white wool and a length of gold Lurex thread between the two layers of card across the centre of the 8. Tie the top section with Lurex thread and the bottom section with wool. Cut and remove the card carefully.

**7** Trim the snowman into shape and make a hanging loop with the left-over gold Lurex thread.

**8** Stick the felt eyes and mouth on to the face. Fold and glue the nose in half and stick it firmly into the face. Fringe the ends of the scarf and tie it around the neck.

**9** To make the hat, oversew the short edges of the side strip together to make a tube. Oversew the tube on to the brim and oversew the top circle on to tube. Spread glue on to a piece of braid and wrap it around the hat. Make a hole on one side at the top of the hat and thread the end of the hanging loop through.

**10** Stick the hat firmly on the snowman's head at an angle. Squash the top down slightly.

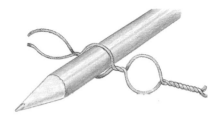

Form the gold wire spectacles round a pencil.

**Safety specs**
If there are going to be young children around over the holiday or you are making the Santa for a bazaar, use gold Lurex thread for the spectacles instead of wire. Both characters are decorations rather than toys, and are not suitable for young children.

## SANTA

### Materials
Red, pink and white DK knitting wool
Scraps of black, red, white and pink felt
Scrap of gold braid or ribbon
Gold Lurex thread
Thin card
Latex adhesive
2 small pieces of thin wire, sprayed gold

### Preparation
**1** Cut out 2 figure-of-eight shapes as for the snowman.

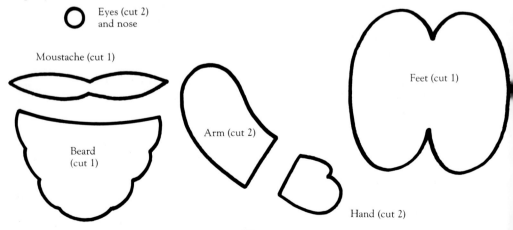

Eyes (cut 2) and nose

Moustache (cut 1)

Feet (cut 1)

Arm (cut 2)

Beard (cut 1)

Hand (cut 2)

2 Trace the beard, moustache, feet, eyes, nose, arms and hands from the patterns. Cut out in white, black, red and pink felts. (Refer to the picture.)

3 Cut a $\frac{3}{8}$ × 7in (9mm × 18cm) strip of black felt for the belt and wrap a small piece of gold braid or ribbon around the centre to form the buckle. Stick the overlap at the back.

**Working the design**

4 Make the Santa doll as for snowman (steps 4–7), except that pink wool is used to cover the upper part of the figure-of-eight cards for the face. Red wool is used for the remainder.

5 When the Santa has been trimmed, use a bodkin or a large-eyed, thick needle to thread several pieces of white wool through the head, from one side of the face to the other. Unravel the ends to make crinkly hair and trim to shape.

6 Stick hands to the arms, and stick the arms in place. Stick on eyes, nose, moustache and beard. Wrap the belt around the body overlapping and sticking the ends together at the back.

7 Make a small pompon by winding white wool approximately 35 times around a finger. Tie off the loops, trim and stick to the top of the head.

8 Make a pair of spectacles from thin wire twisted and formed around a pencil. Coat the ends with adhesive and push firmly into the head.

# THREE

# Top Tables

# Table Santa

*Make this large Santa to preside over your Christmas party table and surround him with little presents for your guests. The figure is made from a plastic bottle and a foam ball.*

## Materials
3 litre plastic fizzy drink bottle
4in (10cm)-diameter polystyrene ball
Red, pink and black crêpe paper
Scrap of black paper
8in (20cm) square of black card
Cotton wool
White felt
1 small buckle
Latex adhesive

## Preparation
1 Using a craft knife carefully cut off the top of the bottle, leaving about ¼in (6mm) of the neck still protruding. Cut the bottom from the bottle about 10in (25cm) down from the new top and discard it.

2 Make a circular groove in the base of the ball by pushing it gently down on to the neck of the bottle.

3 Trace the patterns overleaf and make card templates of the beard, moustache, arm and feet shapes.

## Working the design
4 **Face:** Cover the ball by rolling it in an 8 × 15in (20 × 38cm) piece of pink crêpe paper with the grain running crossways. Use a spot of adhesive to secure the overlap at the back – the groove in the ball should be at the bottom – and screw crêpe paper into a twist (like a sweet wrapping) at the top and the bottom.

5 **Body:** Cover the bottle by rolling it in a 12 × 30in (30 × 75cm) piece of red crêpe paper with the grain running crossways. Secure the overlap at the back with dots of adhesive, and tuck the excess paper at the top and bottom inside the bottle, sticking it in place.

6 Spread adhesive on the crêpe paper-covered neck of the bottle and push the head firmly on to the neck so that the neck fits into the groove. The twist of crêpe paper is hidden inside the bottle. Hold it in place until the glue dries.

7 **Features:** For the nose, cut a 2½in (6.5cm)-diameter circle of red crêpe paper. Gather the edge with running stitches. Pull up the gathers, stuff the nose lightly with cotton wool and tie off the thread ends. Stick the nose to the face. Cut ⅝in (15mm)-diameter black paper circles for eyes and use red paper for the mouth. Stick in place.

8 Spread adhesive around the back and sides of the head and apply layers of cotton wool for the hair. Cut the beard and moustache in white felt and cover them with cotton wool. Stick in place on the face.

9 **Hat:** Make a hat from a 9½in × 13in (24 × 33cm) piece of red crêpe paper with the grain running lengthways. Form a tube that fits round the head, overlapping and sticking the short edges together. Cut a thin strip of white felt and stick it round the bottom edge. Run a gathering thread around the top of the hat, pull up the gathers and tie off the ends. Sandwich the ends between two 1in (2.5cm) diameter circles of white felt.

10 Stick the hat to the head, hiding the screw of pink crêpe paper. Fold the top down (see picture).

**11 Arms:** Form a 5in (12.5cm) square of pink crêpe paper into a tube with the grain running lengthways. Cut the hand shape at one end and stick the edges together. Stuff the arm lightly with cotton wool. Make a sleeve from a 6 × 6½in (15 × 16cm) piece of red crêpe paper formed into a tube with the grain running lengthways. Stick strips of white felt around the cuff. Make 2 arms and sleeves.

**12** Stick the arms inside the sleeves and the sleeves to the shoulders.

**Finishing**

**13** Make the cape from a 5 × 20in (12.5 × 50cm) piece of red crêpe paper with the grain running crossways. Stick a narrow strip of white felt along the bottom edge. Gather the top edge and tie the cape around the neck under the beard.

**14** Make the belt from a 2½ × 20in (6 × 50cm) strip of black crêpe paper with the grain running lengthways. Fold it into 3 lengthways so that the belt fits through the buckle. Wrap the belt round the body, securing the overlap with a touch of adhesive.

**15** Cut out the feet shape in black card, touching up the cut edges with black felt tip pen. Stick them to the base. (As plastic bottles vary in size, check that the feet will fit your Santa.)

**Trace these patterns for the Santa. Adapt the feet pattern outline if necessary to fit your bottle.**

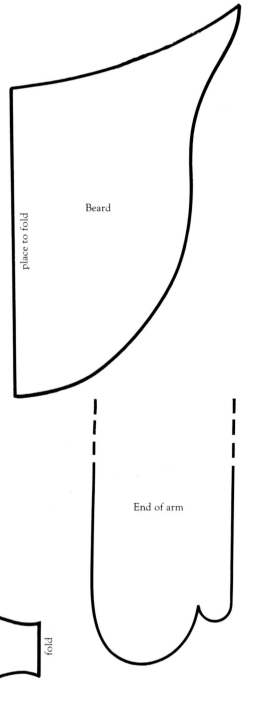

place to fold

Beard

End of arm

Moustache

fold

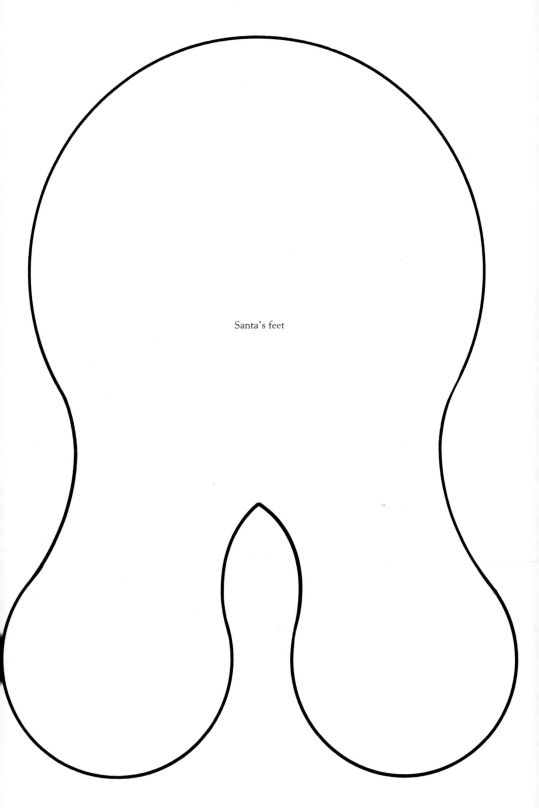

Santa's feet

# Reindeer and sleigh

*A traditional reindeer and a sleigh full of tiny gifts makes an attractive table centre. It could also be used as an advent calendar with twenty-four numbered gifts.*

## Materials for the Reindeer

Two 12in (30cm) squares of thin brown
  card
12in (30cm) square of red paper
Scrap of black paper
6in (15cm) length of gold braid or ribbon
18in (45cm) narrow red ribbon
Small gold bell
All-purpose glue

## Preparation

1 Score across the middle of the brown
card and fold it in half.

2 Trace the patterns of the reindeer's
body, antlers and collar overleaf. (The
pattern for the sleigh and the diagram for
the sleigh base are on pages 50–51.)

## Working the design

1 Transfer the body pattern to the folded card with the line of the back placed along the fold. Cut out. To reinforce the legs, trace the area below the dotted line on brown card. Cut out and stick the pieces to the insides of the legs.

4 To stop the legs splaying out, cut a strip of card $\frac{1}{2} \times 2$in (12mm × 5cm). Score a line $\frac{1}{2}$in (12mm) from each end, fold up to form tabs and glue in position inside the reindeer above the front legs. Repeat for the back legs.

5 Hold the two sides of the head apart in the same way, using a $\frac{1}{2} \times 1\frac{3}{4}$in (12mm × 4.5cm) strip of card. Cut two antlers in brown card and stick them in place. Use a spot of glue to hold the sides of the head together at the nose.

6 Cut small circular eyes in black paper (a hole punch is ideal) and stick them in place. Mark a highlight with white paint.

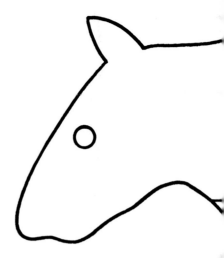

**Trace these patterns for the reindeer.**

7 Cut the collar in red paper. Score on the broken lines and fold to shape. Thread a short length of ribbon through the bell and stick to the bottom of the collar. Carefully put the collar over the antlers, then the head.

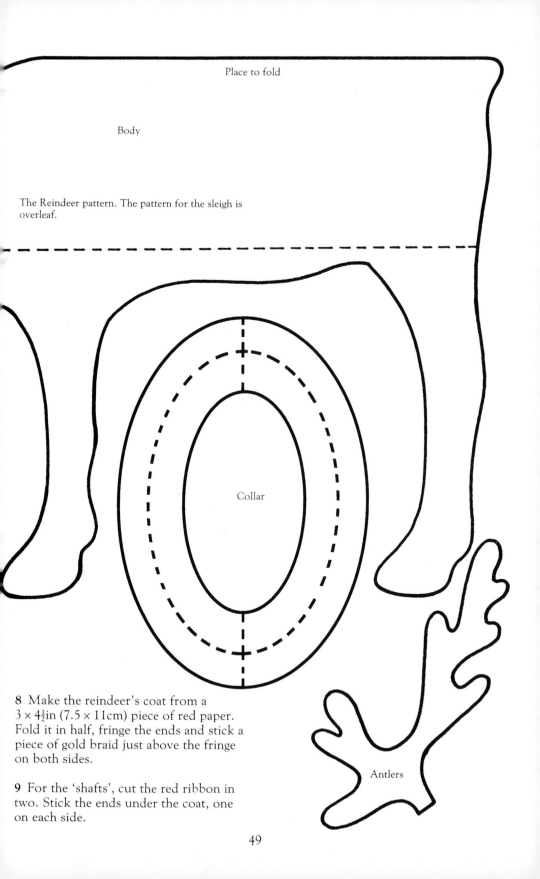

Place to fold

Body

The Reindeer pattern. The pattern for the sleigh is overleaf.

Collar

8 Make the reindeer's coat from a 3 × 4½in (7.5 × 11cm) piece of red paper. Fold it in half, fringe the ends and stick a piece of gold braid just above the fringe on both sides.

9 For the 'shafts', cut the red ribbon in two. Stick the ends under the coat, one on each side.

Antlers

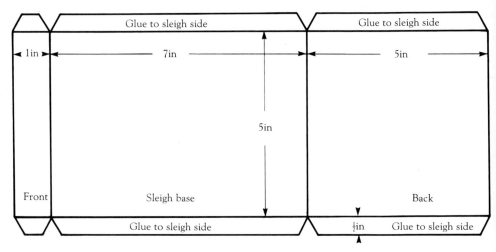

| Glue to sleigh side | | Glue to sleigh side |
|---|---|---|

1in ◄► ─── 7in ─── 5in

5in

| Front | Sleigh base | Back |

| Glue to sleigh side | ½in Glue to sleigh side |

**Santa's sleigh**
Draw the sleigh base from this diagram.

## Materials for the sleigh
11 × 15in (28 × 38cm) piece of gold card
11 × 15in (28 × 38cm) piece of red sticky-backed plastic
5½ × 13in (14 × 33cm) piece of thin red card (or paper)
Scraps of black paper
60in (1.52m) length of gold cord
Mini parcels
Latex adhesive
All-purpose glue

## Preparation
1 Apply the sticky-backed plastic to the back of the gold card.

2 Trace the sleigh pattern and make a card template. Draw a pattern for the base from the diagram.

## Working the design
3 Draw around the template on gold card and cut out both sides of the sleigh, remembering to reverse the template for the other side. Mark the position for the base on the red side (shown as broken lines on the pattern). Cut out the base piece in red card.

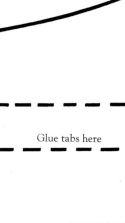

Glue tabs here

**4** Fold the tabs on the sleigh base. Spread glue along the tabs on one side of the base and fix in position to the sleigh side. Repeat with the other side.

**5** Use latex adhesive to stick the gold cord along the edges of the sleigh.

**6** Cut strips of black paper to represent holes between the sleigh and runners (refer to the picture).

**7** Stick the ends of the 'shafts' inside the sides of the sleigh. Fill with tiny parcels.

**8** For parcels, cut small square and rectangular blocks of florist's foam. Wrap in giftwrap paper, tie with narrow ribbons.

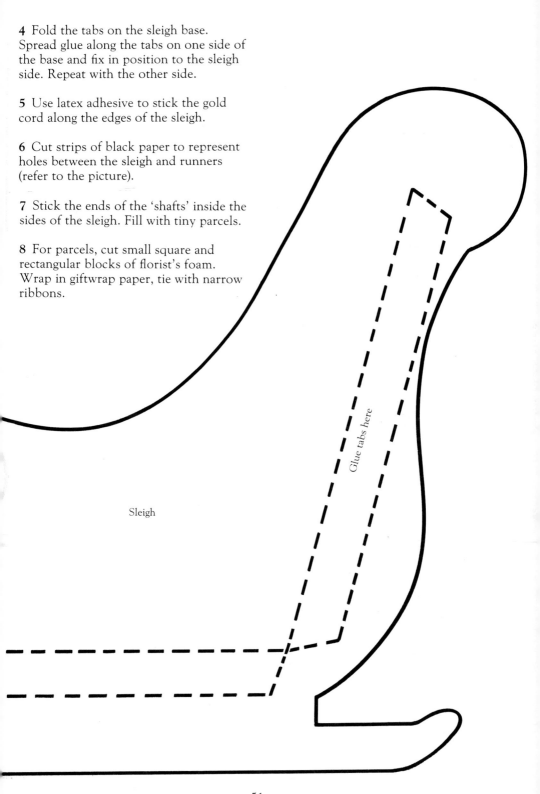

Glue tabs here

Sleigh

# Robins on a log

*The children will love to help make this chirpy choir. The robins are made from painted table tennis balls and pipe cleaners twisted into shape and glued in place.*

**Materials**
5 table tennis balls
Red, white and brown acrylic (or poster) paints
Black pipe cleaners
2½in (6cm)-diameter cardboard tube, 12in (30cm) long
1¼in (3cm)-diameter cardboard tube, approximately 6in (15cm) long
12in (30cm) square of brown felt
8 × 12in (20 × 30cm) piece of white felt
Scraps of beige and dark green felt
Small pieces of black, orange and stiff white paper
2 small red wooden beads
All-purpose glue
Latex adhesive

**Preparation**
1 Using a craft knife, make a hole approximately 2in (5cm) diameter from one end of the large tube, so that the smaller tube will fit into it at an angle. Cut the end off the smaller tube at an angle to represent a sawn-off branch.

2 Pierce 2 holes in each table tennis ball, approximately ¾in (18mm) apart for inserting the legs later.

3 Use scissors to trim the fluff from 10 pipe cleaners to make them thinner.

**Working the design**
4 Cover both tubes with brown felt, sticking the felt down with latex adhesive. Make slits in the felt where it covers the hole in the side of the large tube and fit the smaller tube inside. If it does not fit very tightly secure in position with latex adhesive. Use the pen to mark bark lines on both tubes.

5 Cut circles of beige felt to fit over the ends of the log and branch. Mark growth circles on the felt and glue in position.

6 Cut a piece of white felt to represent snow and stick it in place on the top of the log with latex adhesive.

7 Trace the holly leaf pattern and cut 3 in green felt. Stick the leaves and red bead berries near to one end of the log.

8 Bend each pipe cleaner into legs and claws. Coat the top 1½in (4cm) with all-purpose glue and insert legs into the holes in the table tennis balls. Allow to dry.

Fit the smaller tube into the hole at an angle.

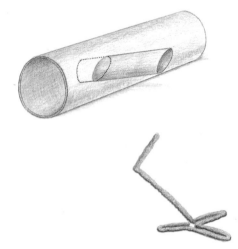

Bend the pipe cleaner to form the robin leg and claws.

52

**9** Trace the tail shape and cut 5 from white paper. Stick the tails in place with all-purpose glue. Paint the robins (see the picture).

**10** Trace the beak shape and cut 5 from orange paper. Cut 10 eyes from black paper. Fold the beaks in half. Stick the eyes and beaks in place. Paint a white highlight on each eye.

**11** Use latex adhesive to fix the robins to the log.

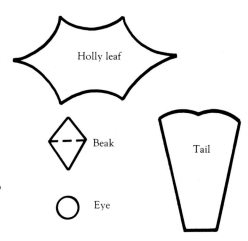

Holly leaf

Beak

Tail

Eye

# Patchwork puff mini-tree

*This lovely little table tree is made from patchwork puffs in printed and plain co-ordinating fabrics. It would make an ideal gift for someone with little space for a real tree.*

**Materials**
12in (30cm) pieces of 45in (115cm)-wide plain fabric in red, green and white
2in (5cm)-diameter plastic flower pot, sprayed gold
Small amount of modelling clay
Small amount of florists' foam
10in (25cm) length of ¼in (6mm) dowel
Tiny gold beads
Small star

**Preparation**
1 Use a pair of compasses and a soft pencil to draw 16 circles on the wrong side of the fabric to the following diameters:
**Dark green:** 12in (30.5cm); 9½in (24cm); 7¼in (18.5cm); 5in (12.5cm); 3in (7.5cm); 2in (5cm);
**Red:** 11in (28cm); 8¾in (22cm); 6½in (16.5cm); 4¼in (11cm); 2½in (6.5cm);
**White:** 10¼in (26cm); 8in (20cm); 5¾in (14.5cm); 3½in (9cm); 2in (5cm).

2 Cut out the fabric circles and make a small hole in the centre of each by folding into quarters and snipping off the point.

3 Put the modelling clay into the flower pot, pushing it well down. Top with florists' foam (the easiest way to do this is to invert the pot and push it down on to the foam).

4 Using a craft knife, taper one end of the dowel. Push the other end into the centre of the pot.

**Working the design**
5 Starting with the largest green circle, gather the edge, pull up the gathers tightly and fasten off the thread ends. Push the resulting puff on to the dowel.

Fold the fabric circles in quarters and snip a hole in the middle.

Push the puffs on to the dowel in decreasing sizes.

6 Repeat with the other fabric circles in decreasing size, in colour order green, red, white. The smallest, last green circle is hemmed before gathering the edge.

7 Trim off any excess dowel at the top with a crafts knife.

8 Make strings of beads and sew around the tree in garlands. Stick a star to the top of the tree.

These little puffs are known as Suffolk puffs and are said to have originated in the English county of that name. In traditional patchwork, they are used to make quilts and coverlets. Puffs are made in plain or patterned fabrics, and are then caught together on the four sides. Sometimes, the puffs are interlined with circles of wool fabric.

55

# Fir cone table tree

*This pretty table tree uses red and green dried plants but the arrangement could be adapted to use any colour scheme. Insert small gold baubles among the foliage for added sparkle.*

## FIR CONE TREE
### Materials
2in (5cm) piece of wood block
¼in (6mm) length of dowel
Fir cones
9in (23cm) florists' foam cone
Bunches of red and green *Achillea filipendulina*
Small amount of dried moss
Florists' binding wire
All-purpose glue

### Preparation
1 Drill a hole in the centre of the wood block. Stick the dowel into the base.

2 Push the florists' foam cone on to the top of the dowel until the cone is approximately 2in (5cm) from the wood block.

3 To wire the fir cones, wrap a 6in (15cm) length of wire around the cone, near its base, and between the seeds. Bring the ends of the wire together and twist into a stem.

## Working the design
4 Insert the wired fir cones in the florists' foam, starting with a ring of them around the bottom and working upwards in a spiral, finishing with a pointed fir cone at the top.

5 Again, starting at the bottom, push pieces of red *Achillea* into the florists' foam half filling the space between the fir cones.

6 Fill in with green *Achillea*.

7 Stick moss to cover the top of the wood block around the dowel.

> **Christmas tree**
> Push sprigs of plastic greenery into the cone tree. Add red berries. Brush the greenery tips with white paint. While still wet, sprinkle on glitter dust.

Push the florists' foam cone on to the dowel rod.

Fill the space between the fir cones with dried material.

# Appliquéd tablecloth

*Your own embroidered festive table linens will be a talking point with friends and family. Appliqué is a simple technique and quick to do – especially when worked with a sewing machine.*

**Materials**

36in (90cm) square of white cotton/
  polyester fabric
8in (20cm) of Christmas print fabric, 48in
  (115cm) wide
4yds (4m) of pre-gathered broderie
  anglaise
Fusible web

**Preparation**

1 Cut 1¼in (3cm)-wide strips of print fabric on the bias to make bias binding. Join these strips to make enough to go all round the cloth.

2 Trace the bow and bell shapes and make card templates. Draw round the templates on the paper side of the fusible web to make 4 bows and 8 bells. Cut out the shapes and iron on to the back of the Christmas print fabric. Cut out.

**Working the design**

3 Round off the corners of the white cotton square. Cut out. Position two bells and a bow in each corner, remove the paper backing and iron in place. Stitch around the shapes using a close zig-zag machine-stitch.

**Trace these shapes for the bell and bow appliqué.**

**Finishing**

4 Fold the bias strip lengthways with wrong sides facing and press lightly. Open out and press the edges to meet at the centre crease.

5 Apply the bias binding round the edges of the cloth.

6 Baste and then stitch or sew the broderie anglaise to the wrong side of the cloth, so that the lacy edge shows on the right side.

58

# Candle arrangement

*This seasonal table centre is made with a pleasing variety of dried material. For a more striking effect, the finished arrangement could be sprayed gold or silver if you prefer.*

## Materials
8in (20cm) oval cork base
Fir cones
Poppy heads
Wheat
Sea lavender
Red broom bloom
Silver and gold spray
2in (5cm) square of florists' foam
Gold candle
Candle holder
Florists' wire
Four 2½ × 24in (6 × 60cm) strips of fabric
All-purpose glue

## Preparation
1 Stick the florists' foam in the centre of the cork base and allow to dry. Insert the candle holder into the centre of the foam.

2 Spread half the fir cones, half the poppy heads and half the wheat on newspaper. Spray gold and allow to dry before turning and spraying the other side.

3 In the same way, spray the other half silver.

4 Wire all the fir cones (refer to Better techniques).

5 Fold the fabric strips lengthways right sides facing, stitch the long seam to make a tube. Press the seam open, turn the tube right side out and press again with the seam at the back. Fold each strip into 4 loops and twist a piece of wire around the middle.

## Working the design
6 Insert pieces of sea lavender and wheat

Form the fabric tubes into 4 loops. Twist wire round the middle, then twist the ends together.

Insert wheat and sea lavender into the florists' foam to extend over the edges of the base.

### Safety tip
Care should be taken with candles as the dried materials are highly inflammable. Never leave lighted candles unattended and replace them with new ones when they have burned to within about 2in (5cm) of the bottom.

60

into the base of the florists' foam so that they extend about 2in (5cm) over the edge of the cork base.

**7** Insert the bows into the 4 corners at the base of the foam.

**8** Gradually build up the shape from the bottom with sea lavender, wheat and broom bloom.

**9** Insert the fir cones and poppy heads at intervals (see picture).

# Presents galore

*Tree cloths are both pretty and practical and this one
with its border of brightly-wrapped presents is sure to get everyone
in a festive mood.*

**Materials**

Piece of green Binca fabric, 44in (112cm)
square, 11 threads to 1in (2.5cm)

Anchor stranded cottons in assorted
bright colours, 15 skeins.

**Preparation**

1 Measure and mark a line 3in (7.5cm)
from the fabric edge all round. Use
basting stitches which can be unpicked
afterwards, or chalk pencil.

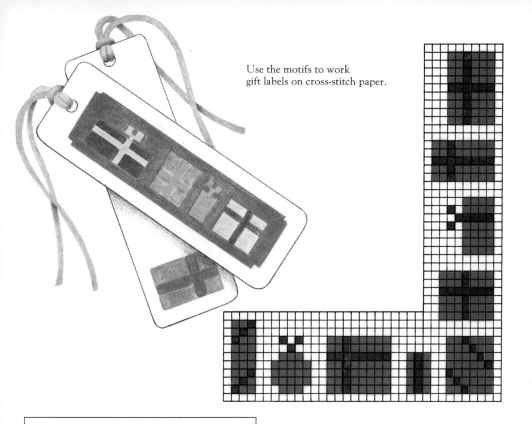

Use the motifs to work
gift labels on cross-stitch paper.

If you don't want to use Binca as a
base for the cloth, use a large-thread,
evenweave fabric such as hessian, in
green or red.

### Working the embroidery

**2** Beginning at one corner and referring
to the chart, embroider a border of
presents along one edge on the marked
line. Use six strands of tread together and
vary the colours at random as you work;
make the colour of each present different
from the ones next to it, with the ribbons
on the presents in contrasting colours.

**3** At the next corner, work the next
present at right angles to the one just
stitched, still working on the marked
line.

**4** Continue working repeats of the
pattern until a border has been worked
round the cloth.

### Finishing

**5** Fold under ½in (12mm) all round the

cloth, press and baste in place. Set the
sewing machine to narrow zigzag stitch,
and stitch the hem. If you prefer, apply a
border of red bias binding to neaten the
edges. Alternatively, sew 1in (2.5cm)-wide
gold polyester/Lurex ribbon to the hem.

Use the gift motifs on cross-stitch
paper to make special Christmas
decorations or unusual gift labels.
Work a row of three or four for a
hand-made Christmas card. You
could also use them as a border for a
Christmas buffet cloth instead of the
holly leaves. If you're feeling
adventurous, work the motif on four
pieces of plastic canvas to be built up
into a three-dimensional Christmas
decoration.

# FOUR

# Children's Holiday

# Gift stockings

*Children love surprises and what could be more exciting than getting a decorated stocking choc full of gifts! Keep the stockings from year to year as part of your holiday festivities.*

## SNOWMAN STOCKING
### Materials
20in (50cm) square each of red felt and white felt
White, black and green stranded embroidery threads
7in (18cm) length of narrow green ribbon
Fusible web
Dressmakers' carbon paper

### Preparation
1 Draw the stocking graph pattern on squared paper. Cut out and chalk around it on red felt for the front. Mark the line of the cuff.

2 Trace the snowman and snowflake. Use dressmakers' carbon paper to transfer 3 snowmen and several snowflakes to the front of the stocking below the cuff line.

### Working the design
3 Work the snowman's outline, hat, mouth, broomstick and scarf outline in stem stitch. Use 3 strands of embroidery thread in the needle.

4 Work the buttons, nose and eyes in satin stitch.

5 Work the brush of the broom, and scarf stripes in straight stitches.

6 Work snowflakes in straight stitches. (Refer to Better Techniques for embroidery stitches.)

7 Cut out the front. Cut a piece of fusible web to the same size and shape, and iron on to the back of the embroidery.

8 Using the pattern reversed, cut out the stocking back in red felt and in fusible web, allowing ½in (12mm) extra on the sides and around the foot. Do not add extra to the top. Iron the fusible web to the back of the felt. Mark the line of the cuff on the felt.

Fold the white felt over on to the fusible surface.

Stitch the front and back together, trim off the white felt edges.

66

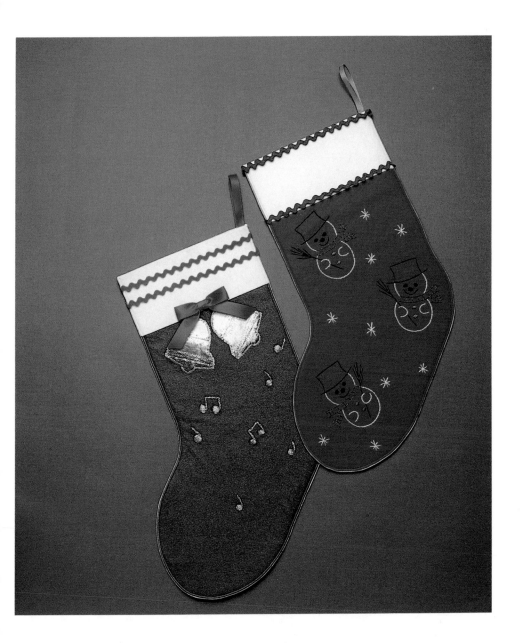

**9** Place the stocking front and back on the white felt right sides up, allowing 3in (7.5cm) extra at the top for the cuff. Remove paper backing and iron in place. Cut out.

**10** Iron fusible web to the red felt on the cuff area of the front and back. Remove the paper backing, fold the white cuffs over and iron in place.

**11** Pin the front to the back with white sides facing. Stitch round the sides and foot using a close zigzag stitch. Cut out close to the stitching.

**12** Fold the ribbon ends under ¼in (6mm). Pin, then sew the ribbon inside the back of the stocking top to make a hanging loop.

## BELL STOCKING
### Materials
20in (50cm) square each of green and
white felt.
Gold braid (or ribbon) for the bells
Gold embroidery thread (or Lurex
thread)
Gold sewing thread
12in (30cm) length of red ribbon for the
bow
7in (18cm) narrow red ribbon
Fusible web

### Preparation
1 Trace the bell and make a card
template. Draw around the shape twice
on the paper side of the fusible web.

2 Iron short lengths of gold braid or
ribbon on to the fusible web, so that the
bell shapes are covered. Cut out each
bell.

3 Chalk round the stocking pattern on
green felt and mark the line of the cuff.

### Working the design
4 Remove the paper backing from the
bells and iron into position just below
the cuff. Using gold sewing thread and
machine zigzag stitch, stitch around the
bells.

5 Trace the notes pattern and transfer to
the stocking. Work the notes in satin
stitch and stem stitch using gold
embroidery thread.

6 Make up the stocking following the
instructions for the snowman stocking
(steps 7–12).

7 Make a ribbon bow and sew in place
above the bells.

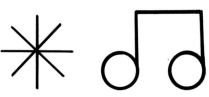

Trace patterns for the Snowman and
Bell gift stockings.

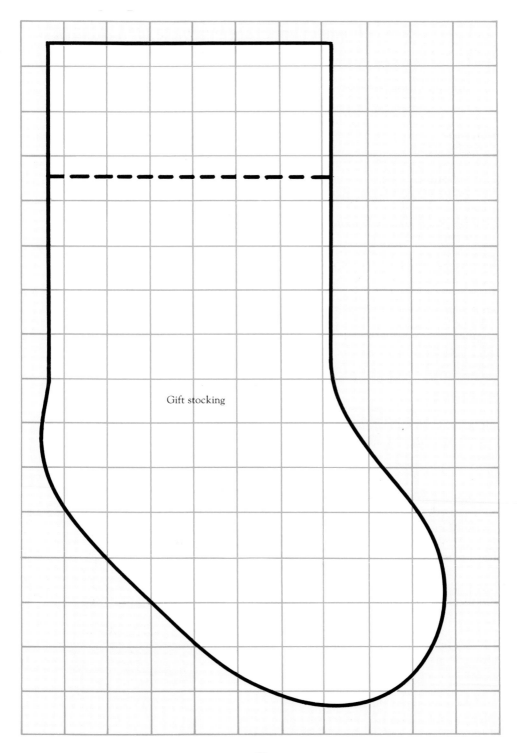

Gift stocking

# Party table clowns

*A jolly clown doll makes an ideal centrepiece for a children's party table and the child's name can be written on a paper strip taped across the front of the doll to make it extra-special.*

**Materials**
**(for each clown)**
1.5 litre plastic fizzy drink bottle
2 litre plastic fizzy drink bottle
2¾in (7cm)-diameter foam or cotton pulp
  ball
Crêpe paper in assorted colours
Tissue paper and felt tip pens for
  trousers
Small piece of millinery buckram for the
  hat
Scraps of black, red and white paper
6in (15cm) square of coloured card for
  shoes
Scrap of cotton wool
Latex adhesive
Soft embroidery cotton

**Preparation**
**1** For the hat, wet a 4in (10cm) square of millinery buckram and form it over the top of a suitable container (for example a spray polish can or deodorant bottle). Allow to dry.

**2** Using a craft knife cut off the top of the smaller bottle, leaving about ¼in (6mm) of the neck still protruding. Cut the bottom from the bottle, 5½in (14cm) down from the new top.

**3** For the baggy trousers, cut the bottom 3½in (9cm) from the larger bottle and discard the top.

**4** Using felt tip pens and a ruler, draw checks on a 4 × 14in (10 × 35.5cm) piece of tissue paper.

**5** Make a groove in the bottom of the ball by pushing it gently on to the neck of the bottle.

**6** Trace the shoes pattern and transfer it to the coloured card.

Form the buckram square over a container then glue into the brim circle.

Push the crêpe paper-covered ball on to the cut edge of the bottle neck.

Wrap the tissue paper round the cut-down bottle for the lower body.

## Working the design

**7 Head and body:** Cover the ball by rolling it in a 6 × 10in (15 × 25cm) piece of pink crêpe paper with the grain running crossways. Use a dot of adhesive to secure the overlap at the back (the groove in the ball should be at the bottom), and screw the crêpe into a twist (like a sweet wrapping).

**8** Cover the body by rolling it in a 8 × 12in (20 × 30cm) piece of crêpe paper (this will be the shirt), with the grain running crossways. Stick the overlap with dots of adhesive at the back and tuck the excess crêpe paper at the top and bottom inside the bottle, sticking it in place.

**9** Spread adhesive on the crêpe-covered bottle neck and push the head firmly on to it so that the neck fits into the groove in the ball. The twist of crêpe paper is hidden inside the bottle. Hold in place until dry.

**10** For the nose, run a gathering thread round the edge of a 1in (2.5cm)-diameter circle of red crêpe paper. Pull up the gathers, stuff lightly with cotton wool and tie off.

**11** Cut eyes and mouth from paper and stick the features in place.

**12** For the hair, cut 4 thicknesses of 4 × 10in (10 × 25cm) crêpe paper with the grain running crossways. Run a gathering thread through all 4 layers along one long edge. Cut a fringe 3in (7.5cm) deep along the other long edge. Spread adhesive on the top, back and sides of the head (around the pink twist of crêpe paper), pull up the gathers, and stick the hair around the head. Make individual strands stick out by curling them around a pencil and spraying with hair spray.

**13 Hat:** The hat is made by pushing the formed top through a circle of buckram for the brim. First, draw a circle on buckram, approximately 1in (2.5cm) larger in diameter than the top of the hat.

Cut out and cut a smaller circle from the centre, large enough to push the top of the hat through. Trim the top of the hat so that it overlaps the brim slightly, moisten this overlap so that it can be moulded around the underside of the brim and stick in place.

**14** Colour the hat with a felt tip pen and glue to the head, hiding the pink twist of crêpe paper.

**15 Arms:** Cut a piece of crêpe paper 2½ × 4½in (6 × 11cm) with the grain running lengthways. Overlap the edges and glue to form a tube. Cut the hand shape at one end and stick the edges together. Stuff the arm lightly with cotton wool. Make a sleeve from a 3 × 4½in (7.5 × 11cm) piece of crêpe paper to match the body. Form into a tube with the grain running lengthways. Round off the top of the sleeves, stick the arm inside. Make 2 arms and sleeves. Stick the sleeves to the shoulders.

**16** Make a bow tie from a 3½ × 6in (9 × 15cm) piece of crêpe paper with the grain running crossways. Run a gathering thread across the grain along the middle. Pull up the gathers and stick a narrow strip of crêpe paper around the middle for the knot.

**17** Wrap the checked tissue paper round the cut-down base of the larger bottle, sticking the overlap at the back and tucking the excess paper into the top. If the bottom of the bottle is shaped, stick the bottom of the trousers to the bottle to represent trouser legs.

**18** Cut shoes from card, and stick to the base of the bottle so that it stands.

**19** A gift can be put inside the base with the clown's body on top. Cut out the braces (suspenders) in crêpe paper and stick them to the trousers, crossing them at the back. If you like write a child's name on a strip of paper or card and glue to the hands.

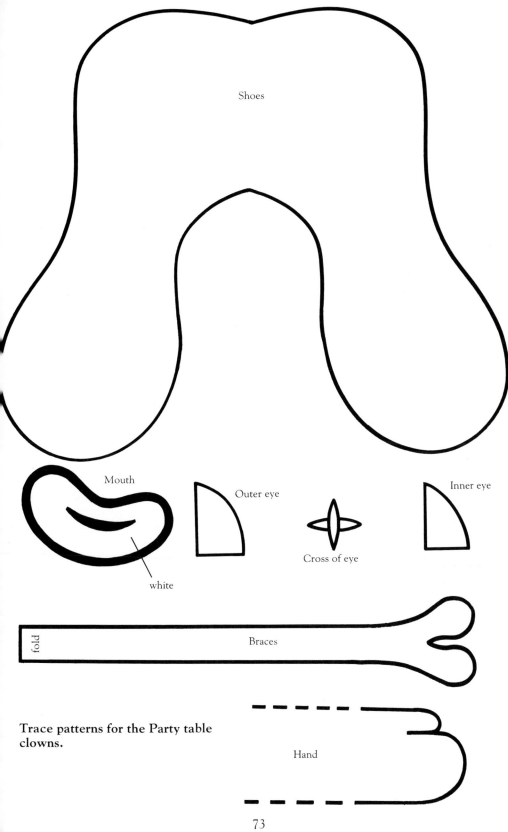

Shoes

Mouth

white

Outer eye

Cross of eye

Inner eye

fold

Braces

**Trace patterns for the Party table clowns.**

Hand

# Advent calendar

*On this advent calendar a parcel is opened each day in December, on the countdown to Christmas day. Each flap opens to reveal a picture or scene cut from an old greetings card.*

## Materials

20 × 21in (50 × 52.5cm) piece of green card
20 × 21in (50 × 52.5cm) piece of green paper
7 × 18in (18 × 45cm) piece of red card
1 sheet of good quality giftwrap with a small pattern
2yds (2m) narrow gold braid
3yds (3m) narrow gold ribbon for parcels, or use a mixture of colours
30in (76cm) of 1in (2.5cm)-wide gold braid (or ribbon)
Self-adhesive numbers, 1–24
Old greetings cards
Paper glue
Latex adhesive

## Preparation

1 To draw the tree shape, measure and mark the centre of the top short side of the green card. Draw lines from this point to the opposite two corners. Cut out this triangle. Use it as a template to draw around and cut out the same shape in green paper and wrapping paper.

2 Find 24 suitable pictures from old greetings cards, and cut them out in squares and rectangles approximately 1–1½in (2.5–3cm).

## Working the design

3 Arrange the pictures on the green paper triangle but do not stick them on. Pencil an outline around each one. Number each picture and the space before removing them. Cut out marked spaces with a craft knife or scissors.

4 Place the green paper triangle (with cut-out holes) on the green card triangle.

Spread a little paper glue on the back of each picture, taking care not to spread it too close to the edges. Stick each picture, through its hole, on to the card. Remove the green paper triangle.

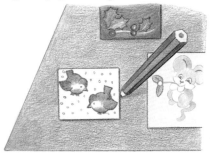

Pencil round the cut-out pictures, cut out the holes.

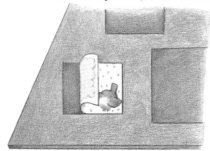

Position the green paper on the green card, glue the pictures in position.

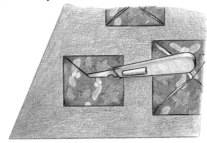

Glue the green paper to the patterned paper; cut diagonals in the patterned paper shapes.

74

**5** Spread paper glue (or spray adhesive) on the back of the green paper triangle, around the edges and around each hole. Stick this to the right side of the giftwrap and allow to dry.

**6** Cut diagonals in the giftwrap. Stick a self-adhesive number in the centre of each parcel, holding the points together.

**7** Spread paper glue on the green card around each picture and around the edges, and stick the green paper with the parcels to the card.

**8** Make a small bow for the top of each parcel and stick in place.

**9** Use latex adhesive to stick narrow braid around the edges of the tree and to make a small loop for the top.

**10** Cut 2 pot shapes from red card. Stick the pot shapes together with the tree positioned so that the top of the pot meets the bottom of the tree.

**11** Decorate the pot with a piece of gold braid and a bow.

75

# Model village

*Children will enjoy making these miniature houses and shops and creating their own winter village. By sticking numbers on the roofs, the village makes an unusual advent calendar.*

## Materials

Cartridge paper in assorted colours
Cotton wool
A clock button
Felt tip pens
Scraps of braid, beads, lace, fabric
   miniature roses etc. Small pictures cut
   from magazines, books etc
Red beads

All-purpose glue
Self-adhesive numbers, 1–24

## Preparation

1 Trace the house pattern on page 79 and make a card template. Cut 24 house shapes from coloured cartridge paper (including the house shape that is part of the church).

**2** Draw the church tower shape on paper and cut out.

**Working the design**
**3** To make each house, mark and score along the fold lines. Fold into shape and stick the tabs.

**4** Make the church tower in the same way. Spread glue on the end of one of the houses and stick to the tower.

**5** Cut out pieces of coloured paper for doors and windows. Use felt tip pens to indicate window frames, curtains etc. Cut pictures from magazines of Christmas trees, people inside the houses. Stick the doors etc, in place. Shop windows can also be made using small pictures cut from magazines. Make square or rounded bay windows using the patterns given. Fold as shown, gluing the tabs to the house fronts.

**6** Spread a little glue on the roofs and along the tops of bay windows. Press cotton wool in place for snow. Glue chimney beads in place and add little flowers and wreaths cut from braid, beads for lights around some of the windows and the clock button to the church tower.

**7** Add cake decoration trees to the display if you like. Put a sweet or candy under each house and fix a self adhesive number to the roof.

Draw interiors on the windows or cut suitable pictures from magazines and glue in place.

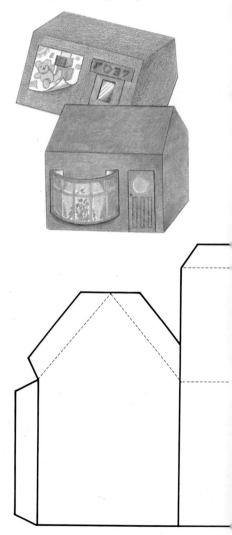

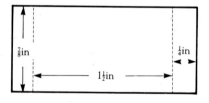

Diagram for the round bay window.

**Church door and window to trace.**

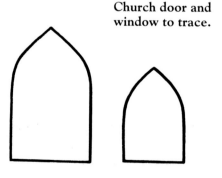

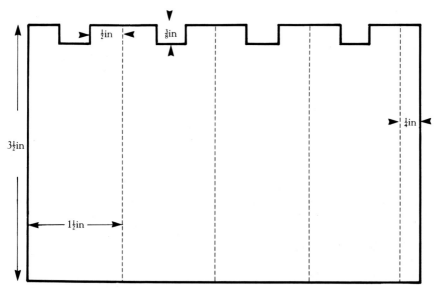

Draw and cut out the church tower
from this diagram.

Diagram for the
square bay window.

Trace this full-sized pattern for the basic
house.

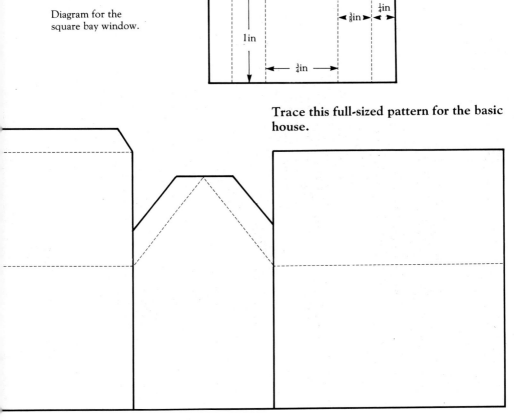

# Easy figures to make

*All the characters are made on corks and wrapped in scraps of coloured paper. This is an ideal holiday project for children but make sure you give them glues specially produced for children.*

## Materials

7 standard-size corks
7 cotton pulp balls $\frac{7}{8}$in (20mm) diameter
Cotton pulp ball $\frac{5}{8}$in (15mm) diameter
Flesh coloured acrylic (or poster) paint
7 × 14in (18 × 35cm) piece of brown card
1 black pipe cleaner
2 white pipe cleaners
Scraps of felt, braid and ribbon
Scraps of coloured paper and tissue paper
Pieces of striped non-woven kitchen cloths
3 beads (or similar) for the kings' gifts
Gold paper star
Black pen
Latex adhesive
Clear sticky tape

## Preparation

**1** Trace the patterns overleaf and make templates. Cut hands from white paper. Paint these, and the cotton balls, pink and allow to dry. Stick a ball to one end of each cork for a head.

**2** Cover the corks by wrapping $1\frac{1}{2}$ × 3in (4 × 7.5cm) pieces of paper round them, sticking the overlap at the back.

**3** Draw the stable pattern (overleaf) up to size.

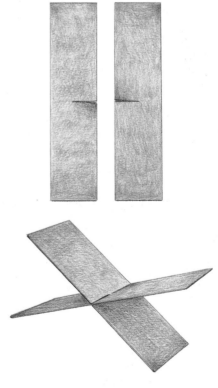

Cut the two pieces of card halfway across then slot together to make the crib.

81

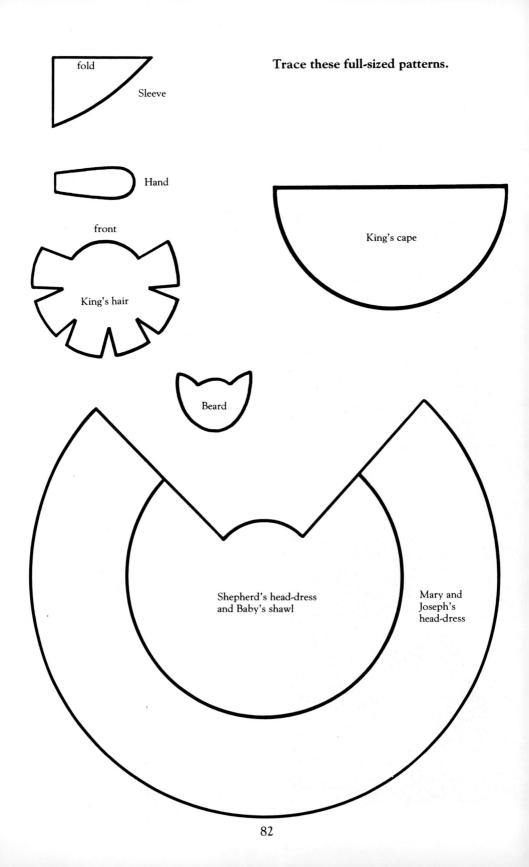

fold

Sleeve

Hand

front

King's hair

Beard

**Trace these full-sized patterns.**

King's cape

Shepherd's head-dress
and Baby's shawl

Mary and
Joseph's
head-dress

## Working the design

**4** Cut sleeves to match the body garment colour, stick hands on the inside. Stick the sleeves to top of the body.

**5** Cut out all the beards and the kings' hair from felt and stick to the heads.

**6** Cut the capes from felt. Wrap a cape around each king, securing with a dot of adhesive at the front. Finish the kings with a piece of gold braid around the heads and a bead stuck to the hands to represent a gift.

**7** Cut the shepherds' and Joseph's head-dress from striped kitchen cloth. Spread adhesive over the top of the heads and stick the head-dress in place. Put dots of adhesive on the inside of the head-dress and press into folds around the body. Stick a piece of narrow ribbon around the head.

**8** Make Mary's head-dress in the same way but using tissue paper.

**9** Draw on eyes and mouths.

**10** Bend a black pipe cleaner into a shepherd's crook for one shepherd. Make a lamb from two white pipe cleaners for the other shepherd to hold.

**11** The manger is made from 2 pieces of card each measuring $\frac{1}{2} \times 2$in ($1 \times 5$cm), which are cut halfway across then slotted together in the middle. Cut short lengths of wool for the straw and stick inside the manger.

**12** For the baby, use the shepherd's head-dress template to cut white tissue. Stick the small cotton ball to the top, wrap tissue around, overlapping and sticking at the front.

**13** Cut the back of the stable from brown card. Cut two $3\frac{1}{2} \times 4\frac{1}{2}$in ($9 \times 11$cm) pieces of card and use sticky tape to attach these to each side for 'wings'. Mark lines on the surface to represent the effect of wood. Stick the star to the top of the stable.

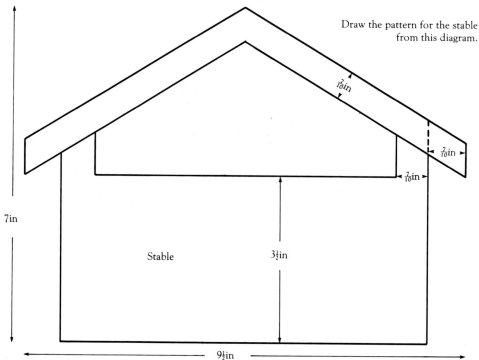

Draw the pattern for the stable from this diagram.

$\frac{7}{10}$in

$\frac{7}{10}$in

$\frac{7}{10}$in

7in

Stable

$3\frac{1}{2}$in

$9\frac{1}{2}$in

83

# Season's greetings

*Make an extra-special Christmas card by embroidering
your own; these three designs are very simple. For variety, work the
designs on different-coloured backgrounds.*

## Materials

### Candy stick card

Piece of pale green Aida fabric, 5 × 4in
  (13 × 10cm), 11 threads to 1in (2.5cm)
Anchor stranded cottons as follows: one
  skein each of 46 red, 230 green, 01
  white
White oval-window card blank.

### Christmas tree card

Piece of white Aida fabric, 5 × 4in
  (13 × 10cm), 11 threads to
  1in (2.5cm)
Anchor stranded cottons as follows: one
  skein each of 244 green, 291 yellow,
  46 red, 89 pink
Red rectangular-window card blank.

# Season's greetings

## Snowflake card

Piece of red Aida fabric, 4in (10cm) square, 14 threads to 1in (2.5cm)

Anchor stranded cotton as follows: one skein of 01 white

White round-window card blank.

## Preparation

1 Measure and mark the middle of the fabric with lines of basting stitches.

## Working the embroidery

2 On all three charts, the middle of the design is indicated with arrows on the edges. This corresponds with the marked middle of the fabric. Using all six strands of thread for the candy stick and Christmas tree, and three strands for the snowflake, work the designs following the charts and keys.

## Finishing

3 Press the finished embroidery on the wrong side with a warm iron.

4 Spread glue around the edges of the window on the inside of the card blank, and position the embroidery behind the window.

5 On the inside of the card, cover the left-hand flap with a layer of glue and fold it over to enclose the embroidery. Leave to dry.

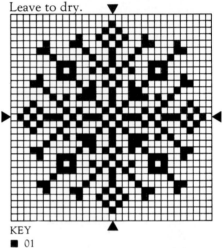

KEY
■ 01

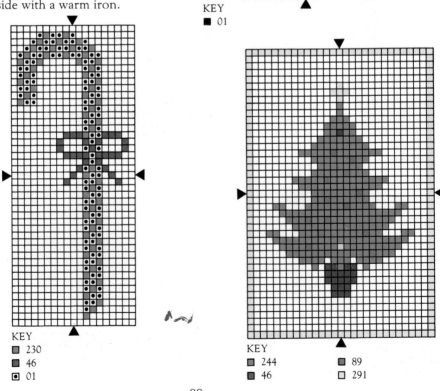

KEY
■ 230
■ 46
◉ 01

KEY
■ 244      ▨ 89
■ 46       ☐ 291

88

Embroider a motif on a
hand-knitted winter cap.

Motifs for cross stitch, like those on
the opposite page, can be used to
decorate not only gift items but are
also ideal for embroidery on
clothing. Cross stitch can also be
worked on knitted items. Simply
position your cross stitches, using
the knitted stitch as a guide. Ready-
made or hand-made garments and
accessories can be personalised in
this way and made to look very
special. Use 4-ply or DK knitting
wool, or tapisserie wool.

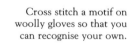

Cross stitch a motif on
woolly gloves so that you
can recognise your own.

Amusing motifs, like the candy stick,
are fun to embroider on casual clothes.

# Embroidered cards

*Anyone receiving one of these cards will want to keep it for ever. They are easy to embroider, even if you have never done this kind of needlework before.*

## Materials
**(for each card)**
Finely woven white cotton fabric
Red, green and gold stranded embroidery
  cotton
Cards with pre-cut windows 2½in (6.5cm)
  diameter
Dressmakers' carbon paper
All-purpose glue

## Preparation
1 Trace the pattern and transfer to the fabric with dressmakers' carbon paper. Follow the colour picture as a guide to thread colours.

## Working the designs
### Bell
2 Using 3 strands of thread in the needle, work the bell and bow in satin stitch.

3 Work the fir sprig in stem stitch with straight stitch fronds.

## Candle
4 Work the candle, flame and holly in satin stitch.

5 Work the fir sprig in stem stitch with straight stitch fronds.

## Making up
6 Cut the fabric to the size of the card.

7 Spread glue thinly round the window of the card on the inside and place the embroidery in position. Press firmly and leave to dry.

8 Glue the return fold around the embroidery and press firmly.

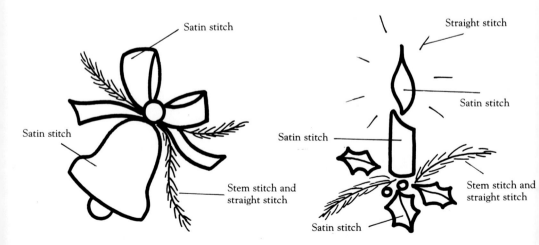

# Robins and snowman cards

*These clever cards are constructed so that the figures are on springs and wobble when they are touched. If you prefer, the pattern could be adapted to a regular card.*

## ROBINS CARD
### Materials
6¼ × 9½in (16 × 24cm) piece of white card
Small piece of light brown card
Scraps of red, orange, black and brown paper
Scrap of green foil paper
2 pieces of florists' binding wire 7in (18cm) long
Clear sticky tape
Black felt tip pen
All-purpose glue

### Preparation
1 Score and fold the white card in half.

2 Use a pair of compasses to draw 2 circles on brown card and 1 circle on red paper, all 1in (2.5cm) radius. Cut out. Cut the red circle in half.

3 Trace the patterns for the holly, beak, tail and branch. Cut out in green foil, orange and brown paper (see picture). Cut out two eyes in black paper and the holly berries in red.

4 To make a spring, wind a piece of wire tightly round a pencil several times so that the coil is about ¾in (18mm) long.

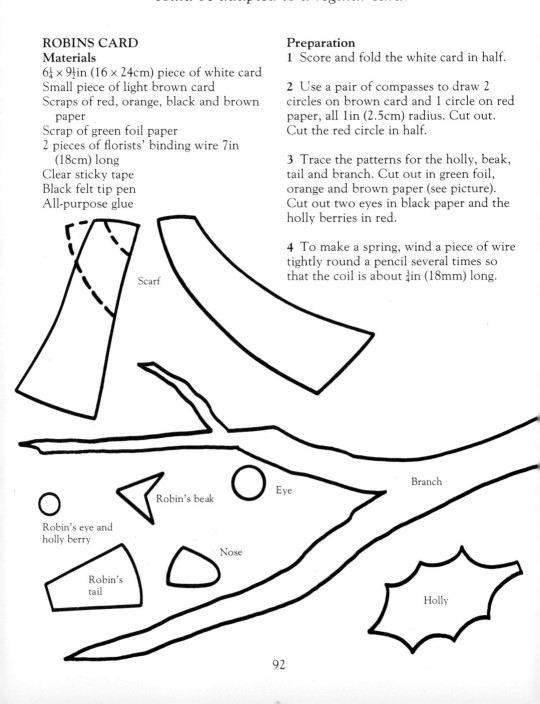

Scarf

Branch

Robin's beak

Eye

Robin's eye and holly berry

Nose

Robin's tail

Holly

### Working the design

**5** Stick the branch across the front of the card.

**6** Stick the red semi-circles to the brown circles for the robins. Stick beaks and eyes in position, then the tails to the back of the robins.

**7** Use a small piece of sticky tape to attach one end of the spring to the centre of the bird's body on the wrong side. Attach the other end to the card so that the robin is positioned above the branch. Repeat with the other robin.

**8** Draw legs and claws.

**9** Spread glue on the back of the holly along the centre and stick to the card, bending the edges of the leaves up slightly. Add the berries.

### SNOWMAN CARD

**Materials**

$6\frac{1}{4} \times 9\frac{1}{2}$in ($16 \times 24$cm) piece of blue card
Small pieces of white card
Scraps of red, orange and black paper
Scrap of red paper ribbon
Silver snowflake, flower or star sequins
2 pieces of florists' binding wire 7in (18cm) long
Clear sticky tape
All-purpose glue

### Preparation

**1** Score and fold the blue card in half.

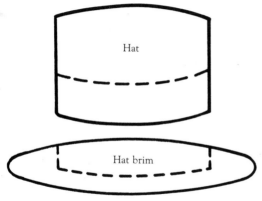

**2** Cut 2 circles from white card, one 1in (2.5cm) radius and the other $1\frac{1}{4}$in (3cm) radius.

**3** Trace the patterns for the scarf, nose, eye and hat. Cut out from red, orange and black papers (see picture).

**4** Make 2 springs, as for the robins card.

### Working the design

**5** Stick the hat, nose and eyes to the smaller circle and the scarf to the larger circle, overlapping the pieces.

**6** Attach one spring to the centre of the body on the wrong side, and the other end to the card about 2in (5cm) from the bottom edge. Attach the other spring to the wrong side of the snowman's head and to the card about $3\frac{1}{2}$in (9cm) from the bottom edge so that it overlaps the body circle slightly.

**7** Stick sequins around the snowman.

# Small things

*Here are some ideas for amusing tree decorations that are ideal for children to make. Five year olds can make the toffee and popcorn garlands, and older children the Christmas pudding ornament.*

**Popcorn garland**
Use plain popcorn and let it cool thoroughly after popping. Thread a sharp, thick needle with a length of narrow satin ribbon. Tie a big knot at the end. Pass the needle through single popcorns, pushing them along the ribbon. They should not touch – let the colour of the ribbon show between pieces. Tie a ribbon loop at both ends to support the garland. Popcorn garlands can be lightly sprayed gold or silver but keep the spraying very light or the popcorns will melt.

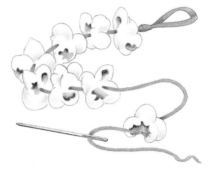

Thread the popcorn on narrow ribbon. Tie loops on the ribbon ends.

**Toffee or candy garland**
Choose sweets that are foil or cellophane wrapped so that they have a glittering effect in the tree lights. Staple the sweet wrappers together at the ends. Tie a loop of narrow satin ribbon at the ends to suspend the garland on the tree.

Staple the wrapped toffees together at the ends.

**Christmas puddings**
**Materials**
Table tennis balls
Brown watercolour paint
White and green felt
Tiny red beads
Gold thread

**Preparation**
1 Paint the ball brown and leave to dry.

Cut white felt to shape and glue to the painted ball. Thread gold yarn through from the bottom end to make a loop.

## Working the design

**2** Cut a 2½in (6cm) square of white felt to shape for the sauce on the top of the pudding. Stick it in place. Cut two tiny green holly leaves from felt.

**3** Sew two holly leaves to the top of the pudding. Sew 2 or 3 red beads to the middle of the holly.

**4** Thread a long, thick needle with gold thread. Push it into the ball from underneath, pull through leaving an end. Leaving a loop, push the needle back through the ball from the top. Knot the threads ends tightly under the ball.

**5** Cut the thread ends to the same length and knot off tightly under the ball, leaving a loop on the top.

---

**Sparkling puds**
If you like a sparkling effect, spray the white felt 'sauce' with a little fixative after cutting it to shape and before sticking it to the ball. Sprinkle on a little glitter dust before the fixative dries.

---

# Better Techniques

❧

*This chapter has some useful ideas for festive trimmings and gift wrapping plus advice on choosing greenery. There are also tips for getting a better finish in needlecrafts.*

## FESTIVE TRIMS
### Making bows
Ribbon bows add the finishing touch to parcels, wreaths, or holiday arrangements and can even be used on their own as tree trims. With a little practice it is a simple matter to make professional-looking bows.

### Ribbon bows
Cut a length of ribbon into two, with one piece slightly shorter than the other. Fold the ends of the longer piece into the middle, overlapping slightly. Sew a gathering thread across the centre and tie tightly. Fold the shorter piece in half around the waist of the bow. Sew in place at the back to form the knot. Arrange the ends neatly and trim to length.

### Fabric bows
Use a strip of fabric twice as wide as the 'ribbon' required plus ½in (12mm). Fold the strip into half lengthways with right sides facing and stitch along the length taking a ¼in (6mm) seam, leaving the ends open. Press the seam open. Turn right side out and press the strip so that the seam is at the back. Form the bow in the same way as for the ribbon bow and finish by tucking in the raw edges. Oversew the ends.

Fold the ends to the middle.

Sew across the centre.

Gather up tightly and tie off.

Fold the fabric round the bow.

Fold the fabric strip in three.

Sew a small piece of fabric over for the knot.

## Tiny bows
Use narrow ribbon and fold into 2 loops, crossing at the centre. Dot latex adhesive at the points where the ribbon crosses and hold the bow in place until it is dry. Trim the ends. A small piece of ribbon can be folded and glued around the waist.

## Florist's bows
These can be made from ribbon or fabric. Fold a length of ribbon in three. Pinch the middle tightly to form the bow. Bend a piece of florists' wire over the pinched middle. Twist the ends together. Pull the loops of the bow into shape.

Bows with more loops can be made in the same way by increasing the number of folds.

## Gift ribbon
Gift ribbon that sticks to itself when moistened is used to make decorative rosettes and bows. Use single colours or mix two or three shades together.

## Rosette
This bow can be made with woven gift ribbon also. Loop the ribbon into several figures-of-eight, tie in the middle with another piece of ribbon. Spread out the loops. Fish-tail the ribbon ends.

This design can also be turned into a star by cutting each of the loops and fish-tailing the ends.

## Daisy
Cut 4 pieces of gift ribbon about 8in (20cm) long. Lay the pieces in a star shape. Moisten and join at the centre. Bring the ends up and fasten together. Moisten the inside of the ball shape and push the top and bottom together firmly until they stick.

## Chrysanthemum
Cut $\frac{1}{2}$in (12mm)-wide gift ribbon into 16in (40cm) lengths. Cut the strips down the middle. Moisten the ends of strips and join them. Turn the ring into a figure-of-eight, moisten to hold the shape. Join 2 figure-of-eights with glue. Make more figure-of-eights and add them, laying them first one way, then the other until a chrysanthemum has been formed. You will need about 14 to get the effect.

Fold the ribbon in three.

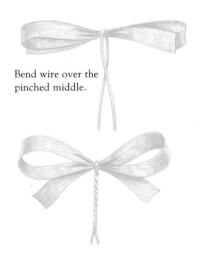

Bend wire over the pinched middle.

Twist the wire ends together.

## GIFT WRAPPING

Wrapping plain boxes is an art in itself and lovely effects can be achieved quite simply through the careful choice of paper and ribbon.

### Square or rectangular box

Make sure that you have enough giftwrap paper. If necessary, tape sheets together. Use a solid glue stick (or double-sided tape) for sealing edges. Transparent adhesive tape always shows and can look messy.

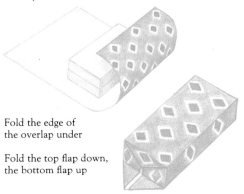

Fold the edge of
the overlap under

Fold the top flap down,
the bottom flap up

Lay the box on the wrong side of the paper. Bring up the sides and then trim the overlap to about 2in (5cm). Fold the edge of the overlap under. The paper should extend over the ends a little more than half the depth of the box. Glue or tape the overlap down. Fold in the sides first, then the top flap down and the bottom flap up. Glue, or fasten with a piece of double sided tape placed under the flaps so that it does not show.

### Round boxes

Trace the bottom and top of the box on the wrong side of the paper. Cut out 2 circles. Measure the depth of the box and the circumference. Cut a piece of giftwrap paper to the box depth measurement plus 1in (2.5cm) with 1in (2.5cm) extra on the length for overlap. Place the paper round the box, fold under the edge of the overlap and glue. Snip into the extra paper at the top and bottom edges of the box to make tabs. Fold them in. Spread glue round the edges of the two paper circles and press them on to the tabs.

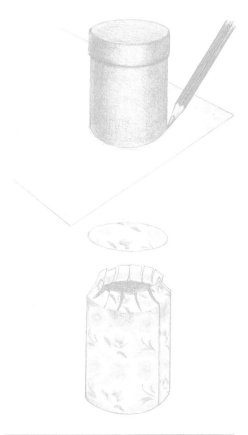

### Large square boxes

Cut and tape paper round the box. Fold and tape the overlaps on to the box top and bottom. Cut paper for the box top and bottom. Tape in place to cover the overlaps.

If you are constantly using a tube of quick-drying glue for a project, choose a nail which fits tightly into the nozzle and knock it through a small piece of hardboard. When not in use, place the nozzle of the tube over the nail. This seals it temporarily and the glue is ready to use when you need it.

## Wrapping plants

Plants in pots are welcome and popular gifts and are not difficult to package attractively. You need a large sheet of stiff card, coloured on one side or with giftwrap paper laminated to it. Stand the pot in the middle of the card on the wrong side. Hold a ruler against the pot on four sides and mark the card. Join the marks and pencil the square. Remove the pot and score along the lines of the square. Next, measure the height of the pot and the plant together. Mark this measurement out from the sides of the square. Draw lines from the corners of the square to the marks. Cut out. Punch a single hole in each point about ⅔in (18mm) from the tip. Stand the pot on the pencilled square, fold up the four sides and tie the box together through the punched holes with ribbon. Tie more ribbons with streamer ends to cascade down the sides of the box.

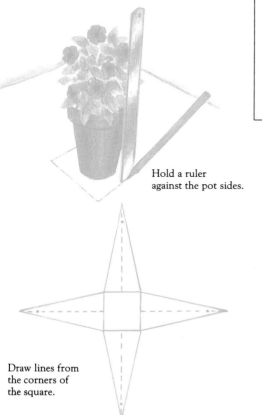

Hold a ruler against the pot sides.

Draw lines from the corners of the square.

## REMOVING GLUES

Adhesive manufacturers will always help with advice about solvents for their products and some will supply these solvents direct if you write to them. In general, the first step in glue first aid is to scrape off any deposit and then proceed as follows:

**Clear adhesive:**
On skin, wash first, then remove any residue with nail varnish remover. On clothing or furnishings, hold a pad of absorbent rag on the underside, dab with non-oily nail varnish remover on the right side.

**Adhesive tape residue:**
White spirit or cellulose thinners may do it. Or try nail varnish remover. Adhesives vary and you will have to experiment.

**Latex adhesive:**
Lift off as much as possible before the adhesive hardens. Keep the glue soft with cold water and rub with a cloth. Treat any stains with liquid dry cleaner. Scrape off any deposits with a pencil rubber.

Fold up the sides, tie the box together with ribbons.

## BETTER TREES

When buying a tree, check that the needles are not already dropping. Most trees are sold without roots so, when you get it home, saw off the bottom 1in (2.5cm) and stand the tree in a bucket of water, outside preferably, for as long as possible. To display the tree, three-quarters fill a tub with broken pieces of brick, wedge the tree stump in and then fill the bucket with damp sand. Press the sand down well to make sure that the tree is secure and upright.

### Alternative trees

In some parts of the world, trees other than conifers are used for the holiday decoration. Any small green shrub can be used and decorated with tinsel or baubles. The small mini-parcels are ideal for decorating small-sized trees.

As an alternative to a tree or shrub, try the effect of painting bare branches white or silver. Spray with fixative and sprinkle a little glitter dust along the top sides of the branches. Stand the branches in a suitable container and decorate with baubles, bead garlands and small gifts. Branch trees look particularly effective displayed against a mirror. They can also be hung across a wall, suspended on small picture hooks.

### Keeping evergreens

Buy, or cut, evergreens only a day or two before they are needed. Choose foliage which looks glossy and avoid branches with limp or dropping leaves. Cut off the ends as soon as possible and stand the branches in water, preferably outside, for as long as possible. If you are using florists' foam, soak this in water before making an arrangement and then keep it damp over the holiday. Unless there are ribbons or decorations which can be spoiled, spray evergreen wreaths, garlands and arrangements regularly with water, particularly when florists' foam has not been used.

### Wired candles

To ensure that candles can be lifted from candleholders easily, wire the ends like this. Cut 3in (7.5cm) lengths of stem wires and hold them round the candle end, with the ends protruding underneath. Bend the ends under the candle and bind them all together with wire. Insert the candleholder into the florists' foam.

### Placing candles

If lighted candles are left in a draught they will burn too quickly and run on one side. Always place candles where there is no discernible air current and the flame burns steadily.

Hold wires round the candle end.

Bind the wires to hold the candle.

## TABLE SETTINGS

Decoratively folded serviettes and table napkins add a special finish to party tables and buffets. Good effects can be achieved with just a few simple folds.

**Triangle:** Fold the fabric into four then in half diagonally.

**Roll:** Fold the fabric into four, roll it loosely. Tie a ribbon round the middle, or use a plain ring decorated with a few dried flowers or a sprig of silk mistletoe.

**Candle:** Fold the fabric in half diagonally, roll it up tightly from the fold. Fold in half again, bringing the ends up and insert into a wine glass.

**Heart:** Fold the fabric in half then into thirds.

**Fan:** Fold the fabric concertina-fashion. Fold in half and insert the folded edge into a wine glass, spreading the fan over the rim of the glass.

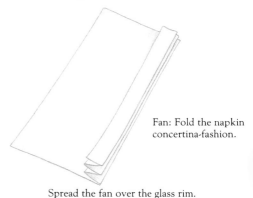

Fan: Fold the napkin concertina-fashion.

Spread the fan over the glass rim.

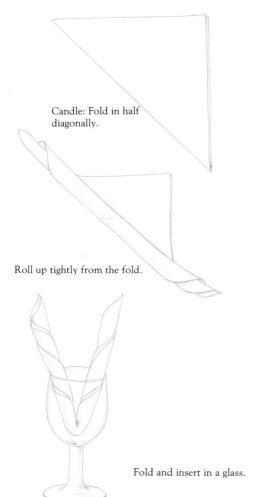

Candle: Fold in half diagonally.

Roll up tightly from the fold.

Fold and insert in a glass.

To make fabric serviettes or napkins, cut plain or patterned fabric into 14 or 16in (35 or 40cm) squares. Work wide, close satin stitch all round the square, about ½in (12mm) from the edge and then trim the excess fabric away after stitching. Coarsely-woven fabrics, such as polyester linen, could be frayed back to make a fringe. Machine stitch all round with an open zigzag stitch about ½in (12mm) from the edge. Snip into the edges all round at 2in (5cm) intervals, then pull out the fabric threads, up to the line of stitching.

**Flower holder:** Fold the fabric in four with the points at the top. Fold each point down in turn towards the opposite corner, finishing with each point higher than the last. Turn the right- and left-hand corners under in thirds. A small Christmas nosegay can be put into the pocket that has been formed.

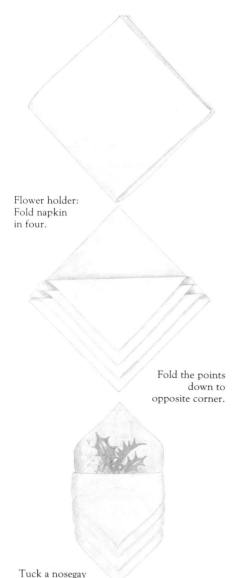

Flower holder:
Fold napkin
in four.

Fold the points
down to
opposite corner.

Tuck a nosegay
into the pocket.

## Checklist
Cutting out scissors
Small, pointed trimming scissors
Old pair of scissors for cutting paper
Glass-headed pins
Assorted sewing and embroidery
needles
Bodkin
Dressmakers' chalk pencil
Tape measure
Ruler
Soft pencils
Felt tipped pens
Sewing threads
Stranded embroidery cotton
Dressmakers' carbon paper
Tracing or greaseproof paper
Florist's wire and wire cutters
Crafts knife
Cutting board
Latex adhesive
Clear, all-purpose adhesive

## Festive tables
For an original and personalized party table, stencil motifs on the tablecloth and napkins. There are a of ready-made stencils in holiday themes in the shops or you can cut your own from stencil blanks. Motifs can be found on giftwrap and greetings cards and there are also some good designs in this book. Retrace the motif on to the stencil blank using typists' carbon paper and cut out with a sharp crafts knife.

Fabric paints are ideal for stencilling and come in a wide range of colours. Stretch the fabric on a surface protected with newspaper. Hold the edges down with masking tape. Use a stubby stencilling brush and mix the paint on the dry side. Tape the stencil in position and dab paint through the holes. Lift the stencil off carefully. Leave each colour to dry before applying the next.

# NEEDLECRAFTS
## Materials and equipment
### Cutting tools
**Scissors:** For basic sewing you need two pairs of scissors. A large pair for cutting out and a small sharply-pointed pair for snipping threads etc. Scissors must be sharp especially when cutting out fabrics. A good pair will give you clean, cutting lines rather than tearing the fabric.

Keep your scissors sharp. Most types can be sharpened on a kitchen knife sharpener. Never use dressmaking scissors for cutting out heavy paper or card because the cutting edge will be damaged, making the scissors useless for cutting fabrics subsequently. Avoid cutting across pins when cutting out as this can damage the blades.

### Measuring equipment
It is essential to have a good tape measure in your work box. This must be made from non-stretch material and have metal ends. The tape will be more useful if imperial measurements are marked on one side and metric measurements are marked on the reverse side. However, when working projects in this book, work entirely to the imperial or the metric measurements. Do not combine the two.

### Marking aids
From time to time you will need to mark the fabric with patterns and designs ready for cutting out. The easiest way to mark outlines on fabric is with a fabric marking pen or with tailor's chalk. Both pens and chalk come in a variety of colours, so choose one a shade darker than the fabric. The chalk will easily brush off the fabric and the pen marks can be removed by washing or, with some types, will disappear after 48 hours.
When you have to mark an appliqué or embroidery design on to fabric, use a sheet of dressmaker's carbon paper.

### Sewing equipment
**Pins:** There is a good variety of pins on the market for different types of sewing.

For most sewing, use a fine, standard length pin (but check to make sure that they are sharp). Blunt pins can snag the fabric, so discard these as you find them in the box.

**Needles:** Needles are divided into groups, depending on their use. For general sewing use 'sharps', available in sizes 3–10 (the higher the number the finer the needle). If you prefer a shorter needle, use a 'between'.

When doing hand sewing, wear a thimble on the middle finger of the sewing hand. This will help push the needle through tough fabrics.

If you have a problem threading needles use a needle threader.

For general embroidery, a mixed packet of crewel needles is sufficient.

### Sewing threads
One of the most important materials in a sewing project is the thread. Always match the type of thread to the fabric, such as silk with silk and cotton with cotton. For mixed-fibre fabrics choose an all-purpose thread. It is important that you match thread to the colour of the fabric. The various brands available all have good ranges of colours from which to choose and, as a general rule, you should go for one in a shade darker than the fabric. If you like to baste seams before stitching them, use a soft, loosely-twisted basting thread.

### Fabrics
When selecting fabrics, remember that closely woven fabrics tend to fray less than loosely woven types. These fabrics are also easier to sew and generally give a good result.

### Interfacing
When a fabric requires extra body, use a layer of interfacing behind the fabric. Interfacing can be simply a layer of a thinner fabric, basted to the top fabric but fusible interfacings are easier to work with. Non-woven fusible interfacings can be bought in various weights.

## Wadding (batting)
Wadding is the layer of fabric that is sandwiched between two other fabrics in quilting. Washable, polyester wadding comes in a range of different weights from light to an extra heavyweight (only used in upholstery). Use a lightweight wadding to give fabric extra body, and the medium and heavyweight versions for quilting, or when an extra layer for warmth is required.

## Decorative trimmings
Ribbons and braids come in most widths and the colour ranges are extensive so it is usually easy to find a good match. Besides plain ribbons in polyester satin, grosgrain, velvet and taffeta, there are printed ribbons, jacquard weaves and a variety of decoratively-edged ribbons to be found. Attach narrow ribbons and braids by stitching them down the centre. With wider ribbons, machine-stitch down both edges, always stitching in the same direction to prevent puckering.

Ready-made bias bindings are useful for finishing raw edges decoratively. These come in cotton or satin in plain colours and are also available in a pretty range of cotton prints.

Lace too comes in a variety of patterns and widths. Choose cotton laces if the item is to be ironed. Pretty broderie anglaise is available flat or pre-gathered, some for insertion and for beading with ribbon.

## PATTERN MAKING
Patterns are generally given in two forms, direct trace-offs and as graph patterns.

### Direct trace-off patterns
To use these, you will need sheets of tracing paper or greaseproof paper. Lay the tracing paper over the book page and tape it down at the edges. Trace the image with a sharply pointed pencil.

Direct tracing from the page.

---

## ENGLISH/AMERICAN GLOSSARY

| English | American |
| --- | --- |
| Basting thread | Soft cotton |
| Bias binding | Bias strip |
| Buttonhole thread | Buttonhole twist |
| Latex adhesive (Copydex) | Latex adhesive (Slomans) |
| Cotton wool | Surgical cotton |
| Elastic bands | Rubber bands |
| Iron-on interfacing | Non-woven fusible interfacing |
| Polyester wadding | Polyester batting |
| Clear sticky tape (Sellotape) | Clear tape (Scotchtape) |
| Cartridge paper | Construction paper |
| Ruler | Yardstick |

Very simple shapes, such as squares or circles, may be drawn directly on to the wrong side of smooth fabrics, using either a soft pencil or dressmakers' chalk pencil. If fabrics are very thin and transparent, full-sized patterns can be direct-traced from the page, using a finely sharpened HB pencil or a coloured embroidery pencil. Another useful marking device is a pen which has air-soluble ink in it. After tracing a pattern the line remains on the fabric for a short time and, usually after sewing, it has disappeared.

## Graph patterns

These patterns are given reduced in size on a squared grid. A scale is given and, to produce a full-sized pattern, you need squared dressmaker's paper marked with squares of the same scale. This paper is sold in large sheets, several to a packet, and can be obtained from dressmaking notions counters.

To reproduce a graph pattern you copy the lines on your pattern paper, square for square.

Enlarging a graph pattern.

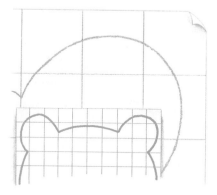

## Preparing patterns

Trace full-sized patterns on tracing paper, spacing pieces about an inch (2.5cm) apart. When a pattern piece is large, it may be split on the page and arrows or dotted lines will indicate where the pieces are to be joined. Trace the largest piece,

move the tracing paper and trace the remaining section.

Some pattern pieces may be shown as one half only. To make a complete pattern, lay the folded edge of your tracing paper against the fold line on the master pattern (this will usually be marked 'place to fold'). Trace the outline, unfold the paper, refold and trace again.

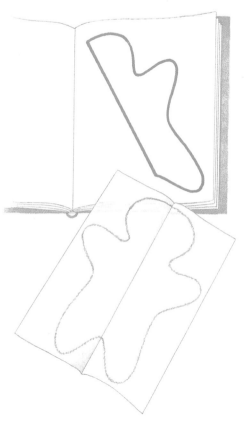

Lay the folded tracing on the half master pattern, trace and open the tracing for the full pattern.

## Transferring patterns

Patterns are transferred to the fabric with dressmaker's carbon paper. This is sold in sheets in packets of three or four colours, red, blue, yellow and white. A sheet is slipped between the pattern and fabric, and then the lines traced over with a tracing tool or an HB pencil.

## SEWING STITCHES

**Basting:** This is a temporary stitch used to hold two layers of fabric together while the permanent stitching is worked.

Fasten the thread end either with a knot or with a double backstitch on the spot. Then take ½in (12mm)-long stitches through the fabrics. Once the main stitching is complete, snip off the end knot (or unpick the backstitches) and pull out the basting threads.

**Running stitch:** This stitch is used for gathering or when stitching fine seams by hand. Work from the right to the left. Begin with 2 or 3 backstitches on the spot. Pass the needle in and out of the fabric, making small, evenly-spaced stitches about ⅛in (3mm) long.

**Backstitch:** This stitch looks like machine stitching when properly worked and is very strong and hard wearing. It is an ideal stitch to use when sewing seams by hand. Work from right to left. Begin with 2 or 3 stitches on the spot then work a running stitch and a space, take the needle back over the space, bringing it out the same distance away.

**Slipstitch:** This is a neat, almost invisible stitch that is used to catch a folded edge in place, such as when applying bias binding, or when joining seam edges from the right side. Work from right to left. Fasten the thread with a knot held inside the fold of the fabric. Bring the needle through and pick up a tiny stitch below the folded edge, then run the needle through the folded edge. Bring the needle through and continue in the same way.

**Oversewing:** Start at the left of the work. Hold the two layers of fabric together and make a double backstitch. Take the needle from the front of the work and insert it from the back. Bring through close to the edge and immediately take the needle over and through from the back again.

Running stitch and gathering

Working slipstitch

## SEAMS

### Seam allowances

Always read through pattern instructions to check whether the pattern includes a seam allowance or if one is to be added when cutting out.

### Pinning and basting

Many needlewomen pin pieces of fabric together and then start machine-stitching without basting. If you feel confident about doing this, by all means work in this way. Basting is helpful when complicated pieces are to be joined and helps you to stitch a straight seam. To baste, thread a needle with soft basting thread and knot the end. Work medium length running stitches just inside the stitching line, removing pins as you go. Finish with a backstitch. After stitching, unpick the backstitch, trim off the knot and pull out the basting thread.

**Plain flat seam:** Place the two pieces of fabric with right sides together. Pin and baste ⅝in (15mm) from the edge. Machine-stitch following the basting line, working a few stitches in reverse at each end of the seam to secure the thread ends. Press the seam open. Neaten the raw edges to prevent fraying with zigzag stitch. Alternatively the edges can be cut with pinking shears.

**Neat corners:** When you are stitching up to a corner, shorten the stitch just before the corner then stop stitching at the corner with the needle in the fabric. Lift the machine foot and pivot the work so that you are ready to work the adjacent side. Work a few stitches with the shortened stitch then adjust the stitch and continue sewing.

### Perfect curved seams

When sewing a curved seam, you will find that you get less drag and distortion on the seam if you start at the halfway point and stitch each side separately.

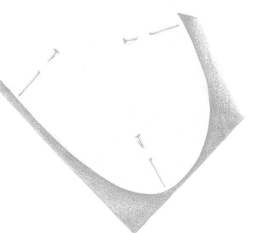

Set pins at right angles to the pattern edge.

### Sewing tip

When instructions indicate that the seam allowance is to be added, first re-fold the fabric, right sides facing. Pin out the pattern. Draw round the outline of the pattern pieces using pencil or dressmakers' chalk pencil. Add all marks. Cut out ⅜in (9mm) from the pattern edge. Unpin the pattern. Baste the fabric pieces together and stitch along the chalked line. This method enables you to achieve accurate stitching and perfect, straight seams.

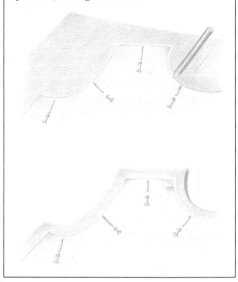

## FINISHING TOUCHES

**Bias strips:** First, find the bias of the fabric. Fold over a corner of the fabric to meet the cut edge, the diagonal fold is the bias of the fabric. Cut through this fold. Use a rule and tailor's chalk to measure strips of the desired width from the diagonally-cut edge.

Pin, baste and stitch strips together along the straight grain ends.

Place the cord centrally to the wrong side of the fabric and fold the strip round the cord. Baste closely against the cord. With a piping foot on the sewing machine, stitch down the strip close beside the cord.

### Binding edges

Bias binding is a neat way of finishing a raw edge as well as adding a touch of colour or pattern. Bias binding can be purchased ready-made in plain coloured or patterned cotton or in acetate satin.

To bind the edge of a piece of fabric, unfold one edge of the binding and lay against the fabric with right sides facing. The crease of the fold lies along the seamline. Pin, baste and stitch in the crease. Trim the fabric edge a little and fold the binding over the edge to the wrong side. Baste, then slipstitch in place, working over the previous stitches.

If the binding is to be topstitched, work the first stage of application in the same way. Bring the binding over the raw edge then baste and machine-stitch in place.

Measure strips from the diagonal cut edge.

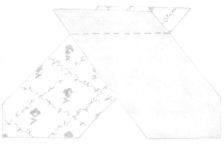

Stitch strips together on the ends.

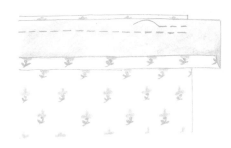

Open the binding and baste, then stitch, along the fold line

Fold over a corner to find the bias.

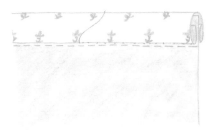

Fold the binding to the wrong side and slipstitch in place

109

**Flat-trim mitring:** Pin the flat trim to the background fabric. Stitch along the outer edge to the corner. Fold the trim back on itself. Pin at the fold. Fold the trim down, creasing the diagonal fold. Press. Lift the trim and stitch on the diagonal. Trim the excess fabric away. Fold the trim back, aligning the lower edge. Stitch on the outer and inner edges.

**Mitred corners:** Turn and press a narrow hem on adjacent sides. Fold and press the corner up. Trim the corner off diagonally, leaving a hem allowance. Press the hem. Fold in and press the sides. Slipstitch the mitred corner.

**Easy appliqué**
Appliqué is a needlecraft that anyone who can sew can master because only simple techniques are involved. You need very little basic equipment, other than that in your sewing basket.

**Slipstitching:** Cut out motifs with a seam allowance. Baste the allowance to the wrong side. Pin the motif to the background, slipstitch along the folded edges.

**Straight-stitch:** Cut out the motif plus a seam allowance. Fold the seam allowance to the wrong side and baste. Pin the applique to the background fabric. Baste, then machine stitch right on the edge of the motif.

**Zigzag:** Trace the motif on the fabric. Machine-stitch along the outlines. Cut out the motif ⅛in (3mm) away from the stitching. Baste the motif to the background fabric. Zigzag-stitch over the motif edges.

Trim the excess fabric away.

Stitch on the outer (above) and inner edges (below).

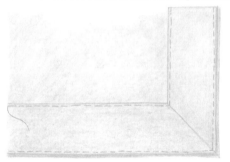

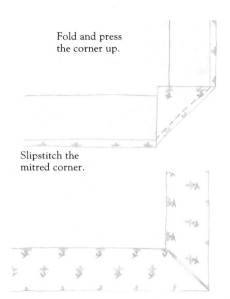

Fold and press the corner up.

Slipstitch the mitred corner.

# EMBROIDERY STITCHES

There are literally hundreds of embroidery stitches to choose from when you are decorating fabric.

## Satin stitch

This is used for filling shapes. Work stitches evenly and so that they touch. Bring the needle through at A, insert it at B and bring it through again at C.

## Straight stitch

Straight stitches can be used to fill shapes or singly. Stitches can also be worked in an eight-point star. Bring the needle through at A, insert it at B and bring it through again at C.

## Back stitch

This stitch, properly worked, looks like machine-stitching and can be used for seaming. Bring the needle through at A, insert it at B and bring it out at C in front of A.

## Stem stitch

This is often recommended for working flower stems and for outlining. Bring the needle through at A, the thread below the needle. Insert it at B and bring it through again at C.

## Chain stitch

Bring the needle through at A and, with the thread below the needle, insert it beside A at B. The thread forms a loop. Bring the needle through at C, pull through gently, ready to start the next chain stitch.

## Detached chain stitch

To work this stitch, from C, work a tying stitch over the loop.

## French knot

French knots are a decorative stitch. Bring the needle through at A, wind the thread round the needle twice and then insert the point at B, close by A. Pull the thread through so that the knot tightens on the fabric surface.

Acknowledgement
The author thanks Heather Best of Best
Floral Designs for the Door wreath on
page 10, the Festive garland on page 12,
the ivy ring in the Doves mobile on
page 16, the Fir cone tree on page 56,
and the Candle arrangement on page 60.